A.C.T.
All Can Thrive

Supporting Mainstreamed Students

Kappa Delta Pi, an International Honor Society in Education, is dedicated to scholarship and excellence in education. The Society, as a community of scholars pledged to worthy ideals:

- Recognizes scholarship and excellence in education;

- Promotes the development and dissemination of worthy educational ideas and practices;

- Enhances the continuous growth and leadership of its diverse membership; and

- Maintains a high degree of professional fellowship.

Kappa Delta Pi invites to membership such persons who exhibit commendable personal qualities, worthy educational ideals, and sound scholarship, without regard to race, color, religion, or sex. The Society's members represent "the best and brightest" in education: from every adult age group, from educators at prekindergarten to college and university levels, and now in more than 90 countries; from education major to classroom teacher to principal to professor of education—comprising a truly intergenerational and international educational honor society.

A.C.T.
All Can Thrive

Supporting Mainstreamed Students

by

Marjorie T. Goldstein, Ph.D.
William Paterson College of New Jersey

and

Susan H. Kuveke, Ph.D.
William Paterson College of New Jersey

Kappa Delta Pi, an International Honor Society in Education
West Lafayette, Indiana
1996

Direct all inquiries to the Director of Publications,
Kappa Delta Pi, P. O. Box A, West Lafayette, Indiana 47906–0576

Executive Director:	Michael P. Wolfe
Director of Publications:	Grant E. Mabie
Editors:	Carol Bloom
	Marji E. Gold-Vukson
	Jennifer L. Kapp
	Victoria Cox Kaser
	Grant E. Mabie
	Leslie S. Rebhorn
Editorial Assistants:	Oke Agahro
	Patti L. Cox
	Jamie Danesi
	Linda A. Heaton
	Nadia Ibrahim
Text and Cover Design:	Angela Bruntlett
Production Coordinator:	Karen L. Klutzke

Library of Congress Cataloging-in-Publication Data

Goldstein, Marjorie T.
   A.C.T.: All Can Thrive: supporting mainstreamed students/by Marjorie T.
   Goldstein and Susan H. Kuveke. p. cm.
   Includes bibliographical references (p.).

   ISBN 0-912099-40-2 (pbk.) $15.00

   1. Mainstreaming in education—United States.
   2. Inclusive education—United States. I. Kuveke, Susan H., 1943– . II. Title.

LC1201.G65 1996

371.9'046'0973—dc21

96-43534

CIP

Printed in the United States of America
FIRST EDITION
01 00 99 98 97 96 5 4 3 2 1

Books can be ordered directly from Kappa Delta Pi for $15.00 plus shipping and handling
by calling 800-284-3167. Quantity discounts are also available. KDP Order Code 508.

Acknowledgments

We completed this project with the help of many people. In particular, our thanks to Michael Wolfe, Carol Bloom, Grant Mabie, Marji Gold-Vukson, and Jennifer Kapp at Kappa Delta Pi for their support, advice, and enthusiasm. On the home front, we are particularly indebted to Herbert Goldstein, Bluma Weiner, Charles A. Weening, Rochelle Kaplan, Norma Goetz, and Michael Reinknecht for their valuable comments and criticisms on early versions of the manuscript. We also want to acknowledge the outstanding direction we were given by our team of anonymous reviewers. Their recommendations were substantive and contributed greatly to improving the original document. We, however, take ultimate responsibility for the resulting document.

Marjorie T. Goldstein
Susan H. Kuveke

Reviewers

Mark Alter
Chair, Dept. of Teaching
  and Learning
New York University
New York, New York

Judith A. Charland
Lecturer—Center for
  Educational Studies
  and Services
State University College
Plattsburgh, New York

Marilyn Dysart
Resource Teacher
Miller Middle School
Marshalltown, Iowa

Thomas W. Jones
Professor of Education
Gallaudet University
Washington, D.C.

D. Kim Reid
Professor of Education
University of Northern
  Colorado
Greeley, Colorado

Keri Robertson
Special Education Teacher
Vinton Elementary School
Lafayette, Indiana

Terri A. Ward
Facilitator, Florida
  Inclusion Network
Department of Education
Daytona Beach, Florida

Contents

List of Figures

Introduction

Dear Readers:

In the best of all possible worlds for educators, as in Garrison Keillor's imaginary Lake Wobegon, every child is "above average." What wonderful news for the teachers in Lake Wobegon! In the real world, however, challenges are the order of the day, and nowhere is that truer than in today's schools. Whether you teach at the elementary or at the secondary level, you probably have a pretty good idea of who most of your students will be and what their general learning and behavior characteristics are. It is likely that your class will be a mix of children who differ in gender, ethnicity, culture, socioeconomic status, and ability. Of these differences, ability differences—with emphasis on wide variations in students' performance and how to deal with them in the classroom—are the focus of this guide.

A few fundamentals can help you get started: First of all, think positive! Take advantage of the staff development opportunities that come your way whenever possible, and find supportive colleagues with whom to share the experience. Especially important, know that you are not alone. You are not expected to have all the answers. Seek help as soon as you realize you need it, and you'll do just fine.

Part 1:
Setting the Stage
for Special-Needs Students

Chapter 1

Placement Considerations for Special-Needs Students

When regular-education teachers were asked to reflect candidly on the experience of having students with disabilities in their classrooms, the reactions were mixed. This was true whether respondents were male or female, whether they taught at the elementary or secondary level, and whether they were veteran or first-year teachers. Reactions also were mixed regardless of whether the student's degree of disability was mild, moderate, or severe. The comments shown in figure 1-1 on page 3 are a sampling of their responses—perhaps you share some of the same feelings. These reactions mirror results reported in the research literature (Hasazi, Johnston, Liggett, and Schattman 1994; Semmel, Abernathy, Butera, and Lesar 1991).

Currently, it seems evident that we lack consensus among frontline, regular educators about their roles in educating students with a wide range of abilities in their classrooms. At the same time, while student variability and diversity have always characterized schools in the United States, what was a trend has become, in recent years, the norm. Political, economic, and social factors help to explain the shift. For example, as the world changes politically, families from many countries and cultures have sought residence in the United States, and their children will be educated in the nation's public schools. Economically, families of limited means have less money available to provide learning opportunities and experiences for their children, often resulting in reduced preparation for school and learning. Also contributing to student diversity are social and legal changes, as when the courts uphold the civil rights of children with serious illnesses to be educated in the schools and to have social contact with peers. Special education placements further add to the mix of students in regular classes, as large numbers of children with mild, moderate, and severe disabilities enter the schools.

Never before have educators been asked to do so much with and for

Figure 1-1 ——————————————————————————————————————

Overheard in the Teacher's Lounge

I've really seen growth in that student.

I'm not qualified.

Can my principal make me do it?

Not in my classroom!

It takes time away from working with the other students.

I enjoy collaborating with colleagues.

What will happen to the other kids in my class?

Don't they have rights too?

When I have a say in what happens, it works well for the students.

I like the challenges!

I'll do it, but I need support!

I have enough trouble with 35 "normal" kids.

OK! Where do I start?

I'm not trained to teach handicapped children.

My whole class benefitted!

students who exhibit such a wide range of academic, social, psychological, and medical needs. And never before have teachers' attitudes and values received so much attention.

Legal Actions Influencing Individuals with Disabilities

In 1975, Congress passed Public Law 94-142. The Education of All Handicapped Children Act (EHA), as this law was called, guaranteed every child—regardless of the type or degree of disability—access to a free and appropriate public education in the least restrictive environment. In 1990, the law was reauthorized as Public Law 101-476, the Individuals with Disabilities Education Act (IDEA). These laws, along with related social legislation like Section 504 of the Vocational Rehabilitation Act of 1973 (Public Law 93-112), have become a driving force in eliminating human and architectural barriers. In addition, the Americans with Disabilities Act of 1990 (Public Law 101-336), which extends opportunities to take part in all aspects of work and social life, has provided a foundation that supports full participation for individuals with disabilities.

These congressional acts have opened school doors to millions of children who previously had been excluded because of their disabilities. Individuals deemed eligible to receive special education and related services are classified using these terms: mentally retarded, learning disabled, seriously emotionally disturbed, hearing impaired, visually impaired, orthopedically impaired, other health impaired, and persons with autism or traumatic brain injury.

It is interesting to note that, from 1975 to 1990, the language of the law changed so that "the handicapped" became "individuals with disabilities." This change was not law-related—instead, it reflects shifting social values and attitudes that are evident in both the professional literature and the popular press. In the popular press, for example, references are often made to people with disabilities as being "physically, socially, or mentally challenged" or "differently-able." Seemingly, the move toward a "people first" rather than a "defect first" philosophy reflects attempts to focus on the concerns of people with disabilities rather than on their deficits alone.

Nowhere is the shift more evident than in the ways professionals interpret the least restrictive environment (LRE) clause of P.L. 94-142 (20 U.S.C., section 1412 [5][B]), amended by P.L. 101-476, IDEA, which states that "to the maximum extent appropriate, children with disabilities . . . are educated with children who are not disabled." Key legal provisions that contribute to structuring an appropriate education for students with disabilities are (1) placement in the least restrictive environment (LRE), with its implications for placement procedures, and (2) development of an individualized education program (IEP).

The Least Restrictive Environment (LRE)

LRE refers to the educational setting in which the instructional needs of a student with a disability can be met "appropriately"—in ways that help the youngster attain the goals of education. To be an appropriate setting, the LRE must foster, to the maximum extent possible, the child's interactions with regular-education peers.

By law, school districts must ensure that a continuum of placements is available to meet the needs of all students with disabilities. Of necessity, this continuum is varied, extending from in-district regular- and special-education classrooms to public and private special schools, hospitals or institutions, and home instruction, as shown in figure 1-2 on page 5. IDEA, the 1990 amendments to EHA, further broadened the concept of LRE to incorporate education delivered to students not only in schools but also in work and community settings.

The Individual Education Program (IEP)

Regardless of the philosophical approach to placement, even students who share the same placement show marked differences in their physical, learning, language, social, and behaviorial characteristics. Thus, following

Figure 1-2 ——————————————————————————————————

Educational Service Options for Students Who Are Exceptional

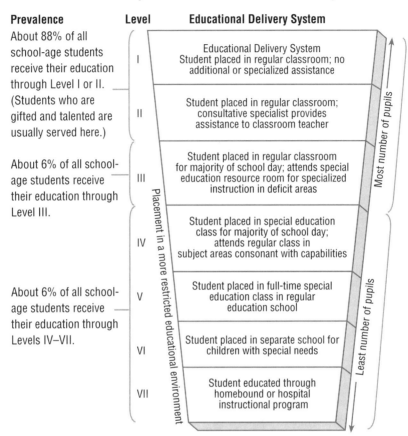

Prevalence

About 88% of all school-age students receive their education through Level I or II. (Students who are gifted and talented are usually served here.)

About 6% of all school-age students receive their education through Level III.

About 6% of all school-age students receive their education through Levels IV–VII.

Level — **Educational Delivery System**

I — Educational Delivery System Student placed in regular classroom; no additional or specialized assistance

II — Student placed in regular classroom; consultative specialist provides assistance to classroom teacher

III — Student placed in regular classroom for majority of school day; attends special education resource room for specialized instruction in deficit areas

IV — Student placed in special education class for majority of school day; attends regular class in subject areas consonant with capabilities

V — Student placed in full-time special education class in regular education school

VI — Student placed in separate school for children with special needs

VII — Student educated through homebound or hospital instructional program

Placement in a more restricted educational environment

Most number of pupils

Least number of pupils

Professional Responsibility

Levels I–III

Regular education has primary responsibility for student's educational program. Special education is support service designed to facilitate student's success in educational mainstream.

Levels IV–VII

Special education has primary responsibility for student's educational program.

From M. L. Hardman, C. J. Drew, and M. W. Winston, *Human Exceptionality: Society, School, and Family.* ©1996 by Allyn and Bacon. Adapted by permission.

placement, law dictates that an IEP be prepared for each student. Developed by a team of school professionals in collaboration with the child and his or her parent(s), the IEP begins with a written plan, typically stated as educational objectives that reflect the student's unique educational, social, and emotional needs. The IEP is implemented according to the plan. At least once each year, the IEP is reviewed and progress is used as the basis for revising and updating it. A complete reevaluation of the student is conducted at least once every three years.

Although IEP formats differ from state to state, as well as from district to district within a state, the content of the IEP is governed by provisions in IDEA (300.346) to include:

- the student's current levels of educational performance, including academic, social, vocational, and self-help skills;
- the special education and related services required by the student, including a statement describing the extent to which the student will participate in the regular education program;
- the annual goals and short-term instructional objectives designed to meet the goals;
- the start date for delivery of services, as well as the duration of services;
- the criteria, procedures, and schedules to evaluate (at least annually) the extent to which the goals and objectives contained in the IEP are being met; and
- for students at age 16, or earlier if necessary, a transition plan stating the services needed to prepare the student for the transition from school to post-school experiences.

Placing the Special-Needs Student

This section will discuss the procedures typically followed when making decisions about the placement of the special-needs student. It also will identify ways in which placement is affected by interpretation of the least-restrictive-environment clause in The Education of All Handicapped Children Act.

A Step-by-Step Plan for Placement

Identification, referral, evaluation, classification, and placement are the procedures that, together, provide access to education for people with disabilities. Identification is accomplished when Child Find and other agencies assist schools in identifying infants and children with disabilities who live in the community. Not surprisingly, the more severe the condition, the easier a child is to find. When a formal referral is made, the child's parent or guardian is informed (in the native language) and must agree to proceed. By law, parents (or their surrogates) are included in every educational decision point in the school experience for a child with a disability.

Following referral, a preplacement evaluation is conducted by a team of professionals using an array of nondiscriminatory, multidisciplinary procedures that include both formal and informal assessments. While team composition differs from state to state, members typically include a school administrator, psychologist, social worker, educational evaluator, and teacher. The team draws together all available information as a basis to consider whether or not the child has a disability. Of course, conducting an evaluation of a child does not assure that he or she will automatically be classified to receive special-education services.

If evaluation results indicate that the child has a disability and requires special education, a meeting is convened with the parents (and, ideally, the student) for the purpose of classification. In this meeting, the type and severity of the child's disability are identified, as well as the child's resulting educational needs, including related developmental, corrective, or other supportive services that are needed to help a child with a disability benefit from special education. These services may include (but are not limited to): special transportation; medical, psychological, social work, and/ or counseling services; physical and/or occupational therapy; audiology; speech pathology; recreation (including therapeutic recreation); and parent counseling and training (IDEA, 300.16). Historically, it was necessary to classify students before they could obtain special education and related services. Presently, however, some schools are exploring new ways to provide needed education and other services without labeling students unnecessarily.

When it is agreed that special education is required, placement occurs in one or a combination of educational settings in which the student can receive an appropriate education individualized to meet his or her needs. Students' particular learning characteristics, in addition to their educational, social, and emotional needs, guide placement decisions. The pivotal question is: "In what setting or combination of settings will the student attain the goals of education to the maximum possible extent?" Once there is agreement concerning the student's primary placement and the amount of time he or she will spend in other educational settings, the decisions are entered into the student's IEP, which is completed following placement.

Fulfilling the LRE Mandate

Despite the language of the law, professionals differ in their interpretations of LRE, and the term has generated controversy from its inception. Many interpret the LRE as a continuum of different educational settings— placement alternatives that provide an array of programs and services to accommodate the different educational needs of students with disabilities. Others believe that the LRE offers a rationale for placing students with mild disabilities in regular classes. Still others use the term to support the placement of all students—regardless of the type or degree of their disability—in the same neighborhood school and classroom they would attend if they were not disabled. As a result, three broad approaches dominate today's discussions of LRE: mainstreaming; the regular education initiative (REI); and the inclusive schools movement (ISM).

Mainstreaming. Students with disabilities who spend most of their instructional day in self-contained special classes are candidates for mainstreaming. Some think of mainstreaming as a practice identified by the amount of time students with disabilities attend regular classes. One difficulty with this approach is that it focuses on students' physical presence in the classroom but may neglect what the students are actually learning.

In an effort to connect mainstreaming to instruction, Gottlieb, Alter, and Gottlieb (1991, 97) described mainstreaming as "the process of developing a special education *instructional* program for academic or social purposes (or both) designed to accommodate a handicapped youngster in a regular education classroom for some part of the school day." Thus, student participation in regular education goes beyond selecting each child's educational setting to considering ways in which an appropriate instructional program and related services can be provided with least disruption for the student. Such a view of LRE recognizes that individual differences among students with disabilities often result in students' requiring different educational settings to secure an appropriate education.

Goldstein (in process) has identified the necessary elements of an appropriate education as the instructional content, methods, materials, technologies, services, and facilities to support the instructional process, and the systematic evaluation of student learning outcomes. These elements must be responsive to students' learning characteristics and their maturational needs and consistent with the goals of education.

The Regular Education Initiative (REI). Frequently credited with breathing life into the REI, Madeleine Will (1986), then assistant secretary for the U.S. Department of Education's Office of Special Education and Rehabilitative Services, characterized regular education and special education as dual systems that were unsatisfactory. She targeted pullout programs—in which students with disabilities received instruction outside regular classes (typically in resource rooms)—as particularly inadequate, noting that students were frequently exposed to inconsistent or disconnected instruction that did not improve their academic performance.

To remedy the situation, Will called for a merger between the two systems. From this critique has grown a movement to reform regular and special education by restructuring education to be more responsive to the needs of all students.

Many have referred to the effort to reform special-education services for students with mild and moderate disabilities as the REI (Reynolds, Wang, and Walberg 1987). A central assumption of the REI is that students fail because of deficiencies in the school rather than because of deficiencies in the individual. Thus, because all children differ from each other, every effort must be made to keep all children in regular education and to provide whatever supports they need within that setting before other settings are considered. Typical supports include the use of pre-referral strategies, consultation between regular and special educators, and in-class support provided by special educators in the regular classroom.

As with mainstreaming, teachers involved with the REI recognize that the ways in which all students differ from each other may have educational consequences that require alternative methodologies, materials, and even placements. Hence, using the premises of REI as a guide, the regular class is viewed as the most desirable placement for students with disabilities, all things being equal. However, there is no assumption that all things are always equal. Instead, the regular class is recognized as the placement of choice when it reflects a suitable setting in which the student can progress academically, socially, and emotionally.

Inclusive Schools Movement (ISM). Professionals, parents, and students who favor inclusion believe that all students—regardless of the type or degree of disability—should be educated in the regular education classroom in the neighborhood school they would have attended if they had no disabilities (Stainback, Stainback, and Ayres 1996). The philosophy that undergirds ISM reflects an emphasis on protecting the civil rights of children with disabilities—a movement fueled by an awareness of the need to protect the rights of all citizens in an increasingly diverse society. Those who support ISM say that all children's educational and social needs can be met in the regular classroom, and that through inclusion it is possible to achieve both equity and excellence in today's schools. Some states and school districts now mandate such inclusion.

Placement options are not stressed in ISM, because all students are placed in regular classes. Instead, efforts that were previously directed toward considering placement alternatives are redirected toward identifying and delivering the curriculum, services, and supports each student needs in the regular classroom.

Understanding In-District Placement Options

While the range of special-education placement options extends to educational settings outside the school district, the great majority of students with disabilities are educated in the district in which they live. The in-district placement options shown in figure 1-2 on page 5 present a continuum based on the extensiveness of special education and related services available in each setting. The following discussion amplifies the description of the in-district educational settings and provides student vignettes to elaborate more fully these ideas.

Self-Contained Special Class (Level V). Regular education is organized by self-contained classrooms such as first grade or fifth grade. Similarly, self-contained classes in special education deliver specialized curriculum and related services to students with disabilities who require significantly different instruction from the regular-education program. Alternative curricula are devised and implemented for these students. In states and districts in which the self-contained special class is a placement option, classes may be organized according to disability category (learning disabilities, mental retardation); within categories by degree of disability (mild, moderate, severe); or across categorical lines by degree (mild disabilities, which could include students with mental retardation, learning disabilities, and emotional disabilities).

Students may spend from half a day to the full school day in a self-contained special class. The amount of time varies according to each student's specific curriculum, individualized instructional needs, and related services requirements. When extensive interventions are required, it is realistic to provide small-group instruction in self-contained special education settings.

For example, a school committee labeled Roy, a second-grade student, emotionally disturbed after all efforts to keep him in regular education had been exhausted. The intensity and duration of his acting-out behaviors pointed to the need for a behaviorally-based program to meet his needs. He has just been placed in a self-contained special class, and no recommendations have yet been made for him to participate in any instruction in regular education.

Self-Contained Special Class (Level IV). Mainstreaming occurs only when a student's primary placement is a self-contained special class. When there is speculation that a student might benefit from instruction or socialization in a regular classroom, decisions are made based on the responses to questions like these:

- Why do we want to mainstream this student?
- In which instructional areas can the student benefit from mainstreaming? Academics? Nonacademics, like music or art or physical education?
- Will the student benefit educationally from the placement?

When the placement team, including the parent(s) and child, arrives at recommendations concerning a student's readiness for mainstreaming, the student's IEP is amended accordingly. The nature of the program to be provided, the amount of time the student will spend in the regular-education setting, and the ways in which progress will be evaluated (and by whom) in the regular-education setting are all specified. Concurrently, this information is communicated to the school personnel who will be involved in implementing the mainstream program.

Here is an example of academic mainstreaming. After a year in a self-contained special class, Bart had begun to improve control of his personal behavior and showed significant educational progress in math. At his annual-review conference in May, Bart's performance was reported at the high second-grade level. As a result, the members of the school's placement team recommended that Bart be mainstreamed into Mr. Grow's third-grade class for math starting in the fall. They chose math because it was Bart's strongest subject, and they recommended starting with a single mainstream experience, so that Bart would not be overwhelmed. After discussing the possible placement with Mr. Grow, it was formalized as part of Bart's IEP, with a preliminary review to occur after one month in Mr. Grow's class.

Nonacademic mainstreaming works somewhat differently. Mary was classified as a student with a communication disability and mild mental retardation, following her placement in a preschool handicapped class for a year. She is now nine years old and has attended a self-contained special-education class for the past three years. Intellectually, Mary functions at a preschool level, although she has shown progress each year. Physically, she is close to the norm for her age. All members of the placement team (professionals, parents, and Mary) agree that she should be mainstreamed into a physical education class, with age-appropriate peers, that meets three times a week. They believe she can function in this setting and that she will benefit both from the socialization opportunities that such a setting offers and from the exposure to fluent language use by peers. Once the mainstream PE teacher is consulted and agrees, the recommendation is formalized as part of Mary's IEP, with the condition that her progress be reexamined at the end of a three-month period.

Resource Room (Level III). Students who attend special-education resource rooms or centers receive most of their instruction in the regular class each day, as stated in their IEPs. Resource rooms or centers are pullout programs, in which classified students receive specialized instruction for a specific period of time each day or week. The instruction provided either supplements and reinforces instruction the child receives in the regular classroom or replaces it entirely. For example, an elementary-level student might attend the resource room daily for instruction in reading and language arts to augment and support the reading program provided in the regular classroom. At the high school level, students assigned to the resource room may receive support in one or more subjects or replacement instruction as an alternative to the regular-class curriculum. When replacement instruction is provided, the student's performance is graded by the resource-room teacher and, if the course is passed, the student earns credit toward high school graduation.

It is worth noting that not all instruction provided in the resource room focuses on academics. Some students need extra help to develop study skills, organizational skills, or other skills that supply needed foundations for learning. These supports also are offered as aspects of resource-room instruction.

As an elementary school example, the primary language spoken in Roberto's home is Spanish, and he seems to think primarily in that language. For the past three years, he has attended a bilingual class where he made limited progress in his command of English. At the end of last year, his teacher referred Roberto for special-education evaluation because of difficulties she noted with reversals and spatial relationships. On the basis of the evaluation, Roberto was classified as having a learning disability. He was placed in Ms. Praiseworthy's regular fifth-grade class and was assigned to attend Ms. Helpful's resource room one hour each day to receive additional instruction and support in the specific areas noted in his IEP.

At the high school level, resource rooms may serve in different ways. Pat, a student with mild mental retardation, has received special-education services since she started school. In the elementary grades, she attended self-contained classes. Now that Pat is in high school, she has been placed in a regular-education homeroom and attends regular-education elective courses in child care, career education, and psychology, with the teachers modifying both the curriculum and the instructional methods for her. She also participates in regular art and physical education classes. In addition, she receives replacement instruction, drawn from alternative curricula, in English, math, social studies, and science from Mr. Best (one of the high school's resource teachers).

Josh, an extremely bright student, demonstrates learning disabilities in the areas of organizational and study skills. Classified while still in elementary school, Josh has received resource-room assistance for the past seven years. He functions well in all his regular-education classes if the teachers adapt their instructional methods to his learning style. The resource-room works with Josh on developing specific organizational and study skills, as stated in his IEP.

Regular Education Class (Level II). Several in-class support options are available in the regular class, depending on the educational needs and related services required by a special-needs student. For students who can benefit from methodological adaptations or modifications to the regular education curriculum, consultation between the regular-education teacher and the special-education teacher determines whether the instructional program is delivered by the regular educator, the special educator, or by a supervised teaching assistant. The special educator who provides in-class support for groups of students (both classified and unclassified) who require adaptations or modifications to their programs customizes the content and instruction to conform to students' abilities. Typically, the special educator teaches individual students or small groups who require more individualized attention, or clarifies and supports the instruction provided by the regular-education teacher. In the regular class, most related services are provided by special-education or health-care professionals.

As a regular-class example, Lawrence, a 13-year-old, has a moderate attention-deficit disorder. He and his parents want him to attend the junior high school in his neighborhood and to have the services of a special educator provided for him in his English and biology classes. According to placement-team recommendations, Lawrence will be grouped with four other students who also need in-class support in the same English class, and three other students (only one of whom is classified) who need additional assistance in biology. The groupings are to foster social integration. Lawrence's IEP stipulates that he is to be included in all regular-education activities and that any necessary support will be provided in the regular-education classroom.

Inclusive education functions differently. Alicia, a 10-year-old girl with Down's syndrome, is placed in the regular fifth-grade class in her school. She walks to and from school with the girl who lives next door to her. She participates in cooperative-learning activities in the classroom and attends art, music, and physical education classes with her peers. The special-education teacher works with the fifth-grade teacher to include Alicia in science and social studies lessons from which she can benefit. Otherwise, the special educator instructs Alicia using alternative curriculum materials consistent with her developmental level. When the teacher is not with her, a teaching assistant helps Alicia to function in the regular classroom.

As school districts explore ways to consolidate programs, some have begun to bring regular education and special education into greater alignment with each other. One result has been that, in increasing numbers, students who display all types and degrees of disability attend regular classes every day. Two or three of these children may have been assigned to your classroom this year.

On the one hand, few actions have as much potential to influence everyday life in your classroom as a special-education placement decision. On the other hand, when students with disabilities are placed in the right classroom for the right reasons with the right supports, teachers often enjoy the expanded opportunities and challenges that emerge as they find new ways to collaborate with colleagues to influence educational planning and instruction. These actions may also result in increased opportunities for students with disabilities to interact with regular-class peers, with the possible outcomes of greater mutual acceptance leading to mutual regard and the growth of friendships.

Chapter 2
Preparing for the Challenges of Special-Needs Students

Regardless of the paths by which special-needs students arrive at your classroom door, their success in functioning in a regular setting will depend on the support structures in place as instruction begins. This chapter will look at ways to prepare for the challenges created by a class of students with diverse needs and abilities.

Premises to Guide Educational Decision-Making

According to the U.S. Department of Education (1993), individuals with disabilities make up almost 12 percent of the school-age population. Most attend their home school district and receive at least part of their education in a regular classroom. In fact, increasing numbers of students with disabilities are attending their neighborhood schools and classrooms.

Managing education in regular classrooms in times when words like "diverse" and "disabled" describe increasing numbers of students requires enormous skill. The premises below provide a common point of departure for the discussion of mainstreaming, the REI, and inclusion. They also offer a context in which to examine educational decisions, especially in situations where neither the issues nor the answers are clear-cut.

The Goals of Education

As a social institution, schools are responsible for socializing each new generation of youngsters. This task is done effectively when the goals of education are met and graduates are equipped with knowledge, skills, and behaviors that enable them to function, contribute, and participate in society. Contribution to society may take many forms; the most important is employment that is compensated at a living wage. The income derived from work enables the individual to take part in social and cultural activities, all of which rest on the ability to function in personal, social, and employment domains.

Individual Differences

While the goals of education apply to all children, we can expect children to meet the goals in different ways and to differing degrees, according to their particular abilities, interests, prior experiences, and learning styles. These are among the characteristics that contribute to the diversity of the school's population and help to account for individual differences.

Placement

Schools offer a variety of ways to accommodate students' individual differences by placing them in classrooms that are designed to respond to their instructional needs. Typically, classrooms are organized by grade level or according to some other criterion—e.g., basic skills instruction, English as a second language (ESL), vocational education, special-education resource center.

Program

Students are assigned to a particular classroom because: (1) the setting is suitable educationally, socially, and psychologically for them; (2) the content and instruction are consistent with student abilities; and (3) the combination of setting, content, and instruction will contribute to students' attaining the goals of education.

Professional Integrity

Regular-education teachers teach the students assigned to their classrooms. While they may not be able to choose their students, teachers do set performance standards that they expect students to meet and make professional judgments about when to modify the standards, once set.

While these premises may assist you in making educational decisions, it is important that the decisions you make are embedded in the professional context in which you function. Thus, you need a clear understanding of your district's philosophy concerning individual differences and the ways your school and district expect you to assist each student in meeting the goals of education. Chapter 7 offers suggested questions with which to evaluate progress toward each of these premises.

The Human Connection

It is important to remember that you are not alone in the responsibility for educating a student with special needs. A team of professionals, including administrators, specialists, and other teachers, works together to ensure the student's educational and social success.

Administrative Support

Recent educational reform and change initiatives (Fullan 1990; Fullan with Stiegelbauer 1991; Muncey and McQuillan 1993) have highlighted the administrator's role in influencing nearly every aspect of life in today's schools. Administrators who organize educational environments in which all professionals contribute to decisions that affect their classrooms create a climate conducive to educating students with disabilities in regular classes (Janney, Snell, Beers, and Raynes 1995; Phillips and McCullough 1990). Just a few of the specific types of support that administrators can provide are:

- setting a tone that fosters the sharing of attitudes, beliefs, and expectations;
- scheduling time for regular- and special-education teachers to meet to discuss, plan, and problem-solve;
- supplying ongoing and relevant staff-development opportunities;
- acting as a bridge between the school's placement team and the parents of a special-needs child; and
- serving as a sounding board when pressures and frustrations begin to build.

One way that administrators encourage collaboration among teachers is by providing them with an essential commodity—time. When teaching schedules routinely include time for regular and special educators to meet together, educators learn to: (1) become good listeners; (2) share information; and (3) make joint decisions about planning and preparing instruction, implementing lessons, and evaluating both student outcomes and teaching-effectiveness outcomes. In sum, they learn to function more fully as colleagues. When school leaders allocate teacher time for collaborative training and planning activities, they demonstrate a commitment to integrating students with special needs into regular education, and they acknowledge this integration as a priority.

Staff-Development Opportunities

Ongoing staff-development opportunities—especially those conducted in a benign setting—frequently provide a rich source of information about the characteristics of students with special needs, instructional strategies, and management models. These opportunities offer the added benefit of experience working with colleagues in collaborative ways (Brandt 1987; Odden and Wohlstetter 1995). For example, staff development can forestall problems that occur when inconsistent or incompatible role expectations lead to conflicts. Some administrators have responded to this by encouraging teachers to develop and circulate job descriptions in an effort to clarify roles. By defining roles and identifying areas of overlapping responsibility as part of a staff-development session, participants can become more comfortable working together. This, in turn, can lead to positive outcomes for the student.

Especially useful as a staff-development device are presentations by teachers who currently are involved in inclusive or mainstream programs. These teachers are in a position to describe difficulties they encountered at the outset, ways in which they overcame problems, and specific instructional strategies they use with students. Reciprocal observations, in which teachers observe veteran practitioners engaged in effective practices in their classrooms, and in which veteran practitioners provide collegial classroom coaching, offer other positive ways for teachers to see colleagues teach and to give and receive feedback. An extra benefit is that these observations can mark the beginning of professional and personal relationships that lead to increased trust and, ultimately, cooperative teaching and learning.

Teachers often report that participating in staff development allays fears, clears up misconceptions, and generates confidence. When staff developers have successfully educated students with special needs in their own classrooms, there is added credibility to the training process. More importantly, Showers, Joyce, and Bennett (1987, 79) reported that "social cohesion and shared understandings do facilitate teachers' willingness to try out new ideas." This openness to new ideas is crucial to building staff collaboration and improving education for students with disabilities.

Team Collaboration

Participants in student-placement decisions typically include school-based professionals, regular and special educators and related services providers, parents, and—whenever possible—the student. With so many people involved, communicating ideas, information, and suggestions accurately and with sensitivity often requires a combination of skill, tact, and persistence. Drawing on research and the positive experiences of both veteran professionals and parents, the following actions suggest ways to begin a planning process that will help integrate students with disabilities in regular classes.

Four Steps to Effective Teamwork. When regular and special educators are actively involved from the time of student referral through the student's placement, they have opportunities to share information in a positive environment. The climate of mutual regard that results creates conditions in which authentic collaboration can thrive. Bergan (1977) developed a widely recognized behavioral approach to consultation—team collaboration. The four steps that lead to effective teamwork are: problem identification, problem analysis, plan implementation, and plan evaluation.

Problem identification occurs when all team members observe both the student and the student's potential class settings to identify the elements of the "problem" that will be addressed through team collaboration. It is also important to review school policies so that recommendations are consistent with established procedures.

The next step is *problem analysis*, during which the team examines relevant classroom variables in relation to the needs of the student. Then, once the classroom setting has been agreed upon, preparation begins for *plan implementation*, using a selection of strategies to facilitate student learning. Following implementation of the plan, *evaluation* occurs at periodic intervals to assess student progress through such means as observation, work samples, checklists, and interviews with the student and significant others (such as parents, family, or friends). When using a team-collaboration approach, the steps are repeated periodically to assure that the student's needs continue to be met.

Questions to Focus Teamwork. The McGill Action Planning System (Forest and Lusthaus 1990) is a highly personalized approach that also focuses on team collaboration as a basis for placing a student in a regular class. Here, the members who will participate in developing the student's IEP—including the student, parents, teachers, administrators, and other relevant professionals—respond to a series of structured questions:

- From your personal perspective, who is this student?
- What is the student's academic, social, and psychological history?
- What are the student's strengths, gifts, and talents?
- What are the student's needs?
- What is your aspiration for the student?
- What is your greatest concern about the student?
- What would be an ideal day for the student?
- What steps must be taken to achieve this ideal?

School teams sometimes invite teachers to complete pre-entry questionnaires, describing their classrooms in detail to assist the team in making placement decisions (Salend and Hankee 1981). Examples of often-asked questions are:

- Is your classroom quiet, moderately active, or very active? In what ways?
- How are transitions made from activity to activity in your classroom?
- What types of assignments do you give?
- What types of work do you expect students to complete while in their seats?
- How much homework do you typically assign?
- What are the ways you use to evaluate student progress?
- What are the stated class rules for behavior? Are there other implied rules?

The team uses the responses to match teacher and setting to the strengths, instructional needs, and behavior of the entering student.

Once the setting has been selected, the team may conduct a classroom variables analysis to gain further insight into the teacher's style, as well as any physical, academic, and social aspects of the classroom environment that may be relevant to the success of the student with special needs (Salend and Viglianti 1982). For example, some students work well under the guidance of a very structured teacher, while others flourish if placed in a class with a more relaxed atmosphere. For still other students, the presence or absence of a competitive environment may be a more important consideration than aspects of the teacher's style.

Teaching Connections

A particularly important element in the collaboration between regular and special educators is the exchange of information about the routines, rules, and rhythms of their respective classrooms. When effective communication occurs, teachers are armed with information that can translate to "survival skills" that students with disabilities need as they prepare for entry into the regular classroom. Ideas about how to accomplish these tasks follow.

Charting daily or weekly routines allows regular educators to communicate the structure of daily life in their classrooms and to alert special educators to events that are part of the weekly schedule, as illustrated in figure 2-1 below. Such a chart helps to convey regular-class activities and provides the special educator with a structure and specific competencies on which to focus. As a communications device, the chart also permits the

Figure 2-1 ⸻

Sample Schedule

Regular Class Daily Schedule	Sara's Schedule
8:30—Opening: Flag, Milk Money, Sharing Circle	Van arrives: 8:25 a.m.
9:00—Reading: Group/Individual Activities	
9:45—Gym: Calisthenics	* Medication
10:30—Written Language (Computers)	

special educator to highlight specific time-relevant needs a student with disabilities might have, like a medication schedule or a regularly scheduled counseling session.

The Classroom Ecological Inventory (CEI) is a highly structured approach used by both the regular-education teacher and the special-education teacher to identify important differences between their classrooms (Fuchs, Fernstrom, Scott, Fuchs, and Vandermeer 1994). The sequence of actions includes observation (the physical environment, teacher/student behavior, posted classroom rules, implied classroom rules, and teacher behavior), interview, comparison of environments, and reconciliation of differences between the two settings. Space is also provided to describe assignments, tests, and student evaluation procedures. By reducing the differences between the ways the "sending" classroom and the "receiving" classroom function, and by handling mainstreaming or inclusion on a case-by-case basis, the authors report an increase in successful student placements in regular-education settings. A copy of the CEI is shown in figure 2-2 on pages 22–24.

To make sure that ongoing communication between teachers continues after the student is placed, an SOS (Something Out of Sync!) form is useful (Safran and Safran 1985). This communication strategy uses informal notes, as shown in the sample form in figure 2-3 on page 25, to alert other teachers when all is not right with a mainstreamed or included student. The immediate response required in this approach ensures that little problems do not become big problems.

For students who are absent from your classroom for whatever reason, what better way to help them reenter than by letting them know what activities took place in their absence? Lazzari and Wood's (1993) "While You Were Out" message form, shown in figure 2-4 on page 25, communicates task expectations, while at the same time letting the students know that they were missed. An added benefit is that the form can be copied and shared with students' other teachers as a communication device.

Figure 2-2 ──────────────────────────────────────

Classroom Ecological Inventory

Special Education Teacher_____Grade___Date_____

Regular Education Teacher_____Number of Students in Regular Class ____

Student _____

Part 1: Classroom Observation

■ Physical Environment

Directions: Please circle or provide the appropriate answer.

1. Is there an area for small groups?   Yes   No
2. Are partitions used in the rooms?   Yes   No
3. Is there a computer in the classroom?   Yes   No
4. Where is the student's desk located? (for example, front of room, back, middle, away from other students, etc.) _____

■ Teacher/Student Behavior

Directions: Please circle the appropriate answer.

1. How much movement or activity is tolerated by the teacher?

                                        Much   Average   Little   Unclear

2. How much talking among students is tolerated?

                                        Much   Average   Little   Unclear

3. Does the teacher use praise?   Much   Average   Little   Unclear

4. Was subject taught to the entire group or to small groups?   Entire   Small

Directions: Please provide an appropriate answer.

5. During the observation, where did the teacher spend most of the time? (for example, teacher modeled the lesson, asked students to work at board, helped small groups, helped individual students)_____

_____

_____

_____

6. What teaching methods did you observe while in the classroom? (for example, teacher modeled the lesson, asked students to work at board, helped small groups, helped individual students) _____

_____

_____

_____

7. How did the teacher interact with students who appeared to be low achieving or slower than their classmates? (for example, helped them individually, talked to them in the large group) _____

_____

_____

_____

Preparing for the Challenges of Special-Needs Students

■ Posted Classroom Rules

If classroom rules are posted, what are they?

Special Education	Regular Education
_____	_____
_____	_____
_____	_____

Is there any other pertinent information you observed about this classroom that would be helpful in reintegrating the student? (for example, crowded classroom)

_____

_____

Part 2: Teacher Interview

■ Classroom Rules

	Special Education	Regular Education
1. During class are there important rules? (Yes or No)	_____	_____
2. If yes, how are they communicated? (for example, written or oral)	_____	_____
3. If class rules are *not* posted, what are they?	_____	_____
	_____	_____
	_____	_____
	_____	_____
4. If a rule is broken, what happens?	_____	_____
What is the typical consequence?	_____	_____
5. Who enforces the rules? (teacher, aide, students)	_____	_____

■ Teacher Behavior

	Special Education	Regular Education
1. a. Is homework assigned? (Yes or No)	_____	_____
b. If so, indicate approximate amount (minutes) of homework, and	_____	_____
c. the frequency with which it is given.	_____	_____

Directions: Using a 3-point scale (1=Often, 2=Sometimes, 3=Never), rate each item according to frequency of occurrence in class. Place an asterisk (*) in the right-hand margin to indicate important differences between the special and regular education classrooms.

	Special Ed	Regular Ed
2. Assignments in Class		
a. Students are given assignments:		
• that are the same for all	_____	_____
• that differ in amount or type	_____	_____
• to complete in school at a specified time	_____	_____
• that, if unfinished in school, are assigned as homework	_____	_____

b. Evaluation of assignment:
- teacher evaluation   _____   _____
- student self-evaluation   _____   _____
- peer evaluation   _____   _____

3. Tests

a. Tests are
- presented orally   _____   _____
- copied from board   _____   _____
- timed   _____   _____
- based on study guides given to students prior to test   _____   _____
- administered by resource teacher   _____   _____

b. Grades are:
- percentages (example, 75%)   _____   _____
- letter grades (example, B+)   _____   _____
- both   _____   _____

4. Academic/Social Rewards

a. Classroom rewards or reinforcement include:
- material rewards (example, stars)   _____   _____

b. Classroom punishment includes:
- time out   _____   _____
- loss of activity-related privileges (example, loss of free time)   _____   _____
- teacher ignoring   _____   _____
- reprimands   _____   _____
- poorer grade, loss of star, etc.   _____   _____
- extra work   _____   _____
- staying after school   _____   _____
- physical punishment (example, paddling) _____   _____

5. To what extent do each of the following contribute to an overall grade? *Estimate the percentage for each so that the total sums to 100%.*
- homework   _____   _____
- daily work   _____   _____
- tests   _____   _____
- class participation   _____   _____

6. Please list skills that have been taught since the beginning of the school year (Regular Education Teacher Only):

Skill	Will Reteach Later?
_____	_____

Figure 2-3 ──────────────────────────────
Something Out of Sync

_____ is having some problems in

_____(Subject Area)

Please _____ work with him/her in the LD room on: _____

_____ contact me to set up a meeting.

Most convenient times would be: _____

_____

Regular Class Teacher

©1985 by PRO-ED, Austin, Texas. Reprinted by permission.

Figure 2-4 ──────────────────────────────
While You Were Out Form

To _____

Date_____ From _____

WHILE YOU WERE OUT

The Class

_____ Read pages _____ in _____

_____ Read pages _____ in _____

_____ Did a written assignment on pages _____

_____ Did a written assignment on a worksheet. _____

_____ Took a test on _____

_____ Listened to the teacher present a lesson on _____

_____

_____ Had a group discussion on _____

_____ Copied material from the board.

_____ Watched a filmstrip or video on _____

_____ Other _____

A=This item is attached   S=See me about this

©1993 by The Council for Exceptional Children, Reston, Virginia. Reprinted by permission.

Figure 2-5 ───

Matching Student Needs to Instruction

Extent of Curriculum Change	Type of Change		
	Instructional Methods	Educational Content	Setting
ADAPTATION of regular education curriculum	X		
MODIFICATION of regular education curriculum	X	X	
ALTERNATIVE curriculum to regular education	X	X	X*

* Students with disabilities who need highly individualized alternative programs have traditionally been educated in self-contained classes. Exceptions occur when students with moderate or severe disabilities are educated full-time in regular classes.

A Curriculum Perspective

With so much variability among students with disabilities, it is no wonder that there are no simple formulas to guide either the selection of suitable placements or the identification of appropriate programs. To assist you in making instructional decisions about students' programs, figure 2–5 on page 26 provides a guide for matching students' learning needs to instruction.

The criterion for decision making is how extensive the curriculum and/or methods changes must be in order for the student with special needs to demonstrate continuing progress toward meeting the goals of education. Specifically, changes range from adaptations of methods of instruction to modifications of instructional methods and content drawn from the regular education curriculum and the use of alternative curricula when it is deemed appropriate. When an alternative curriculum is selected, changes include altering the methods, content, and—frequently—the logistics with which the program is delivered. Ultimately, the extent to which the student's instructional program must be changed is governed by his or her progress toward attaining educational goals.

Curriculum Adaptations

Many students, including those with learning disabilities and emotional disturbances, benefit when teachers utilize tangible activities—like demonstrations and simulations—to augment traditional lecture and discussion methods. Adaptations frequently focus on making instruction more concrete as, for example, when students are given opportunities to "learn by doing" or when they use several senses simultaneously to reinforce what they are learning. Adaptations may also include changing the rate at which instruction is presented, altering the amount of instruction contained in a single lesson, or using available technologies to support student learning. Adaptations represent minimal changes to students' programs and are usually accomplished within the framework of the regular-education program.

Curriculum Modifications

Some students—including those with mild mental retardation—require programs in which both the instructional methods and aspects of the regular-education curriculum are modified to meet their needs. In addition to making methodological changes like those identified above, the instructional content is also modified for these students. Often, the content is distilled and assignments are shortened or otherwise altered to bring them in line with a student's abilities and rate of learning. Even with these modifications, many students with disabilities can benefit from curriculum that draws its content and structure primarily from regular education. Adaptations and modifications to instruction are detailed in chapters 3–6.

Curriculum Alternatives

Students with moderate and severe mental and physical disabilities may require an alternative curriculum in which the content differs from that of the regular-education curriculum by being highly specialized to meet students' particular instructional needs. Alternative programs incorporate the adaptations and modifications noted above while providing students with planned and structured learning experiences that may differ markedly from the regular-education curriculum. Examples of alternative curricula are a developmental progression of content focused on brushing teeth (Lent 1975) and instruction that deals with getting along with others or emotional security and self-expression (Goldstein 1974; 1975).

While regular-education students often learn these types of skills by observing and imitating the behavior of their peers, some individuals with disabilities need a planned program and much practice to master such basic social competencies. These alternative programs are relevant to students' current levels of development; at the same time, they establish foundations for mastering competencies needed to function in—and contribute to—society as an adult.

Most of the time, students with disabilities who require alternative curricula spend correspondingly less time in the regular classroom in order to take advantage of the specialized curriculum and methods provided in a self-contained special class. However, in school districts where an inclusive schools movement (ISM) is implemented, the needed curriculum, services, and supports are imported into the regular classroom and delivered by a special educator or teaching assistant.

The Classroom Connection

Managing instruction begins by creating classroom environments in which students can grow and learn. Attention to physical, behavioral, and instructional aspects of the setting are steps toward creating classrooms in which all students can thrive.

Creating the Physical Environment

When structuring the environment, a starting point is to delineate the various activities in which students will participate. The goal is to arrange the physical setting functionally to maximize learning (Brophy and Good 1986). For example, to accommodate the needs of students with sensory or physical disabilities, it is essential to make the classroom as barrier-free as possible. To accomplish this, it may be useful to grid the classroom on chart paper to visualize and plan individual seat assignments, small group and individual work areas, computer stations, and other learning centers you want to make part of life in your classroom, as well as traffic patterns in the classroom.

Figure 2-6 ─────────────────────────────────
Day-by-Period Tracker

Period	Mon	Tues	Wed	Thurs	Fri
1					
2					
3					

When areas of the classroom are designated for specific activities, you also create a basis for student accountability. As they grasp the classroom's physical layout, students become responsible for their whereabouts at any point in time. For instance, if scheduled for a group-reading lesson, students would have no reason to be in the computer area. When concrete physical cues, like blinking the lights, are combined with verbal directions, students with special needs stand a better chance of being where they are expected to be in the classroom. In addition, using different areas of the classroom

Figure 2-7 ——————————————————————————————————
Period Schedule: Math Class 9:00–9:55

9:00–9:05	Turn in assignments/Review yesterday's notes
9:05–9:40	Instruction: Note-taking
9:40–9:55	Complete practice problems at seat/ Write down homework assignment
9:55	Turn in practice problems/Dismissal

for different activities can give students a "change of scenery" and different classmates with whom to interact.

Because students with disabilities are sometimes scheduled to receive instruction outside the regular class, a handy way to maintain a record of every student's whereabouts for every period of the day is to create a "Day-by-Period Tracker" using a form like the one shown in figure 2-6 on page 28. The completed chart can be duplicated for particularly "mobile" students, with their schedules highlighted as a visual reminder of their personal commitments.

Schedules establish routines, and some students feel more confident when the schedule is posted so they can refer to it throughout the day. With the many different activities that occur each day in most elementary classrooms, a posted schedule can provide an added reminder for those students who forget "what comes next." At the secondary level, teachers can post a period schedule, containing key structures for typical lessons and setting expectations for the class like the one shown in figure 2-7 above.

Seat assignments are an essential part of a smoothly running classroom, because who sits next to whom can make the difference between a calm classroom and chaos (Rosenberg, O'Shea, and O'Shea 1991). Seating arrangements can have added importance for students with special needs, because the youngsters seated next to them may determine their social status in the classroom. For this reason, consider seating newcomers to the class next to especially popular students (after you have cleared it with the popular youngsters, of course). Try a rotating seating chart that puts each student, in turn, next to a student with special needs. Such a strategy can be beneficial to all students and build strong feelings of shared responsibility. Another consideration is that students with disabilities to whom large-group instruction is new may need an unobstructed view of you (and vice versa). Seat assignments may vary by activity in the early grades, by lesson in the middle grades, or by subject at the secondary level.

Assignment folders help some students with disabilities get—and stay—organized. Having their own folders also makes students responsible for keeping track of their assignments and completed work. Some frequently used folder titles are: "(Specific Subject) Seatwork," "Work in Progress," "Homework to Do," and "Completed Assignments." Use a color-code system and store folders in a clearly identified, accessible place to aid students in retrieving folders.

Creating the Behavioral Environment

The physical organization of the classroom helps to communicate your expectations for student behavior. However, explicit rules are often needed as well. Whether generated by the teacher, or by the teacher and class together, "Class Rules" charts frequently are used to convey the ways in which students are expected to behave in the classroom. Class rules are most effective when they are few in number and stated in positive ways that tell students exactly what is expected of them. For example, "Keep your hands in your lap" and "Leave homework in the green basket at the start of each class" are more direct and specific statements than the amorphous "Don't hit" or "No late homework." Creating an environment based on stated rules also gives students authentic preparation for dealing with the laws of the world beyond school.

A few behavioral strategies follow as reminders of those techniques that continue to stand the test of time. For instance, modeling and demonstration are durable teaching tactics that remain effective, especially when coupled with active practice. When it comes to behaviors that are absolutely required in your classroom, some students with disabilities benefit from observing a classmate demonstrate the desired task or behavior, which gives them a concrete model to imitate.

While most students seem able to interpret a teacher's facial or movement cues (especially negative ones) with ease, it may be necessary to specifically teach included or mainstreamed students to "read" the cues you use in your classroom. They may need explicit instruction to interpret your frowns, head-shakes, nods, or other idiosyncratic cues—e.g., flipping the lights to get attention—to behave according to your expectations.

Increasing students' awareness of your behavior also can guide them to increased awareness of their own behavior. A simple self-management system can be effective (Wolery, Bailey, and Sugai 1988). Begin by identifying a desired behavior in simple and observable terms, stating the behavior positively, and communicating your observations to the student. Then, with the student, set a joint goal regarding the sought-for behavior. For example, if Alexandra curses, one way to help her change the behavior is to focus attention on word substitutions. Have her count the number of times she replaces a curse word with another word—e.g., "darn" for "damn." Have Alexandra keep tabs on the behavior, period by period, and chart results at the end of each period. At the end of the day, meet briefly with Alexandra to compare observations and discuss progress.

Students can use these charting activities to become more responsible for their own behavior. Even the teacher can get involved—some teachers have modeled this procedure by counting a behavior they want to change, like the habit of ending sentences with "okay?" Youngsters seem to find this approach especially motivating!

A functional guide for students to use when examining their own behavior is the antecedent-behavior-consequence (ABC) analysis, in which the student first identifies the circumstances and people who were around before and up to the time the inappropriate or undesirable behavior occurred, in an effort to reconstruct and organize the events leading to the behavior (Salend 1994). Next, as part of the analysis, the student defines and describes in detail the intensity and duration of the behavior. Finally, the student considers what the outcomes of the behavior were. The resulting analysis leads the student to set goals aimed at avoiding a reoccurrence of the behavior in the future.

The same analysis can be used to study the effectiveness of a teacher's behavioral strategies. For example, some teachers unconsciously reward negative behavior by giving a child lots of attention for behaving in inappropriate or unacceptable ways. Keep in mind that some students prefer receiving negative attention to receiving no attention at all. If you find yourself rewarding negative behavior, you can alter the situation by modifying the consequences for the behavior; for example, you can ignore a behavior to which you had previously reacted, then praise the student when the appropriate behavior is shown.

When a student experiences difficulty controlling behavior or has a hard time attending to a task, using study carrels to remove a student from the stimulation of the group temporarily can be constructive. In addition, some students appreciate having the option of using a carrel to put themselves into "temporary time out" if the need arises. This option empowers students by giving them greater control of their environment and, ultimately, of themselves.

Creating the Instructional Environment

Knowing where the student with special needs "fits" in relation to the other students in the class can help you create the instructional environment. The student's IEP will help you with this task by identifying the areas in which special education and related services are required; it also will specify whether the student needs interventions to adapt, modify, or replace regular class instruction.

Several familiar classroom interventions that can translate into positive school outcomes for students with special needs are highlighted below. These interventions include general procedures for grouping, pre-lesson management, assignment adaptations, test-taking accommodations, and teaching for generalization.

Grouping Strategies. Research has shown that grouping practices can have a powerful effect on instructional outcomes. In fact, "research on cooperative learning is overwhelmingly positive, and the cooperative approaches are appropriate for all curriculum areas" (Joyce, Showers, and Rolheiser-Bennett 1987, 17). This is especially true if the students work toward unified group goals—working to achieve a common purpose—while

---

Figure 2-8

Cooperative Learning Writing Lesson

"I introduce a writing lesson by telling students on what skills they'll be graded. If the mechanical skill is spelling, a group knows it's responsible for making sure there are no misspelled words in any member's final draft.

"I begin with a brief whole-class discussion or instruction. If I'm doing a lesson on descriptive writing, I might start by showing a painting. We talk about details, colors, and feelings it evokes. Then I show another painting and ask students to list words that come to mind as they look at it.

"I set a time limit for brainstorming, then I ask students to pass their papers around the group. Some kids will have long lists, while others will have only a few words. You'll hear comments like, 'Oh, I didn't think of that.' You'll see eyebrows raise and eyes light up as kids think of new words. That's the point of sharing—to open up students' minds and help them generate more ideas.

"Next, each student writes a topic sentence. Again, there's a sharing of papers and a chance for group members to point out a sentence that seems vague or will be hard to support with details.

"So students proceed from prewriting to first draft in this same way, all done in class, in groups, sharing their work and seeking reactions from one another.

"When it's time to hand in the finished essays, I randomly select one paper from each group to grade, and each member gets that grade. But I only give group grades for practice on a skill. When students have had plenty of work with descriptive writing, I'll give an assignment to be graded individually.

Davis, J. 1992. Transition to teaming. **Instructor: Middle Years** 2(2):16–18.

being individually accountable—every group member must demonstrate learning (Slavin 1989–90).

Teachers start by identifying student characteristics that are important to the group's ability to complete its task and determining whether to group students homogeneously or heterogeneously. Although homogeneous groups have been used conventionally to introduce students to academic concepts, other class activities often encourage heterogeneous groupings for social, behavioral, or academic reasons. In fact, the past decade has seen a great deal of attention paid to promising practices for grouping learners who demonstrate a wide range of abilities. Figure 2-8 below is a typical cooperative-learning lesson, dealing with the subject of writing.

Effective use of cooperative learning does not happen overnight. Edwards and Stout (1989–90) candidly described their early experiences implementing cooperative learning, including the trials and missteps. They share the following practical suggestions to help teachers get started:

- Arrange the physical setting efficiently to minimize unnecessary movement.
- Determine group size: "When in doubt, start small" (40).
- Decide how long groups will stay together, whether for a lesson, a day, or a project.
- Divide group responsibilities.
- Form new groups as needed, and give students plenty of opportunity to get to know each other before initiating assignments.
- Decide when it is appropriate to use cooperative learning and when it is not.

When planning a grouping strategy, several factors must be considered, including students' various learning styles and instructional needs, as well as the amount of information to be communicated and the pace at which instruction will occur. To accommodate students with special needs, it may be necessary to present less information at one time and to include plenty of opportunity for guided practice to rehearse and repeat newly learned material.

One way this can be accomplished is through peer tutoring, in which two or more students group together to learn or reinforce instruction that has already occurred. The relationship between the tutor and tutee is defined by their respective abilities in relation to the particular task, as well as by the objectives to be met as outcomes of their work together. Sometimes there is an even exchange of skills or information among students whose abilities are reasonably similar, which is true with buddy systems. More often, tutoring involves students of unequal abilities—one student already has mastered a skill or concept and attempts to teach or reteach it to the other student. In this case, potential tutors must receive training in how to work sensitively with other students.

Cross-age tutoring involving older students with mild or moderate disabilities tutoring younger children can be an effective grouping strategy. Perhaps several youngsters in your class could participate in a tutoring project with children three or four grades below your level. Being a teacher-tutor does wonders for students' egos, encouraging feelings of competency and success.

Pre-Lesson Management Strategies. How the day's activities are paced also influences learning. For example, provide a balance of active and sedentary activities during the day by scheduling academic instruction and related services to be interspersed with "specials" like physical education, art, music, or computers. This structure allows students to expend excess energy periodically and in appropriate ways, so that they are better able to stay on task for extended periods of sedentary instruction time.

Classroom transitions pose a related scheduling issue, because transitions are the least-structured portions of the school day, with ready-made opportunities for students to misbehave. Therefore, preplanned, predictable transition routines that lead from one activity to another, or are used when students leave or reenter the classroom, can be integral to the success of the instructional program.

At the outset, demonstrating the behavior you expect from students as they move from one activity or subject to another provides the youngsters with a visual model to follow. For some students, added cues might be necessary—for example, a five-minute warning might be announced before the end of the period to give youngsters who need it time to prepare for the transition. Some teachers find that using a stopwatch to practice transition routines is motivating.

Jones and Jones (1986) found that a transition time accompanied by a brief, structured activity helps settle the students and, at the same time, allows for individual differences in rates of "activity-shift" ability. Having students use transition times for two-minute journal-writing activities, for example, gives the time an instructional purpose for which each youngster is accountable. Practicing transitions is time well spent, usually resulting in establishing common expectations for classroom behavior.

Assignment Adaptation Strategies. Teachers most readily agree to adapt assignments for students with disabilities if: (1) the adaptation is unrelated to the learning goal; and (2) a reluctance to adapt the assignment would result in student failure. When it is necessary to adapt assignments, a student's IEP should provide guidance about altering seatwork or homework to take greater advantage of the student's strengths.

Assignments should retain their academic integrity when adaptations are made. However, having a classmate photocopy course notes, assignments, or directions for students with special needs neither compromises the assignment nor permits them to experience failure for reasons unrelated to ability. For example, if a student's IEP notes a weakness in copying from the board, supplying preprinted assignments does not compromise the assignment because writing was not the primary learning objective.

At another level of adaptation, if the class is assigned 25 homework problems, perhaps the student with special needs might begin by being required to complete only 15 problems and work up to completing the full assignment. In fact, some school leaders are beginning to question the need to insist that all youngsters perform the same tasks in the same ways at the same time.

More and more, as educators draw on both the research on multiple intelligences (Gardner 1983; Armstrong 1994) and the expanding literature on cooperative learning (Johnson, Johnson, and Holubec 1987; Slavin 1989; 1989–90), they recognize that students may need a variety of options to meet the same learning objectives in different ways. With this in mind, your local special-education colleague is a good source of ideas about options for a particular student with special needs.

Test-Taking Accommodation Strategies. Test-taking accommodations, like assignment adaptations, are addressed in the student's IEP. Some of the more usual accommodations include giving the student:

• oral rather than written tests;
• extended time to complete examinations;
• a reader to read the test and/or to record answers;
• a calculator; and/or
• a computer or word processor to use, rather than requiring written responses.

It is important to note that at no point do the test-taking accommodations compromise the examination if the test is at the student's ability level.

Teaching for Generalization. One primary goal of schooling is to enable students to generalize the skills and information they learn in school so they can use these same skills and information to solve everyday problems. Most children seem to make connections between what they learn and how the information can be applied to similar settings or events without too much difficulty. However, students with disabilities often have a hard time making these connections (Deshler, Ellis, and Lenz 1996). For them, an important instructional goal is to develop a generalization strategy focused on problem solving and critical thinking.

Students with disabilities often need a great deal of repetition and practice to become competent generalizers. Ideally, instruction should offer students opportunities to learn strategies aimed at helping them acquire new information, relate that new information to prior knowledge, and store and retrieve that information across situations and settings (Deshler, Ellis, and Lenz 1996). When instruction: (1) supplies students with learning strategies; (2) uses content that is relevant from the student's point of view; (3) provides plenty of concrete examples; and (4) promotes immediate practice to reinforce newly learned knowledge, skills, and behaviors, students become more independent learners and gain confidence in their abilities.

Part II:
Teaching and Learning Strategies for Special-Needs Students

Chapter 3

Strategies for Teaching and Learning Language Arts

Being an effective reader is essential for success in most areas of the school curriculum. In fact, the ability to read and comprehend can influence not only academic achievement but a student's self-concept and post-school adjustment as well. Because most students with special needs experience difficulties in reading and/or comprehending content, we have emphasized these areas here.

Where to Start

As noted earlier, curriculum-based assessment is important preparation for instruction. To augment the results from typical assessment procedures used when any new student enters your classroom, we suggest that you conduct a private, oral-reading assessment with the youngster. As the student reads aloud from material targeted at an appropriate level of difficulty (according to the IEP), you can follow along on another copy of the material, noting words the youngster cannot read. As the student reads, try to answer these questions:

- Does the problem lie in an inability to recognize words instantly and automatically?
- What strategies does the student use to analyze unknown words?
- Are there difficulties identifying complex vocabulary words or comprehending vocabulary in specific subject areas?

The same reading passage can be used to assess student responses to comprehension questions targeted at literal, interpretive, and evaluative levels. Analyzing student errors can give you an idea of specific strategies to select. The following are some things to look for, because students with special needs frequently demonstrate one or more of these reading problems:

- poor mastery of instant word recognition that interferes with fluency;
- poor mastery of phonetic and linguistic skills needed for successful word analysis—e.g., sound-symbol relationships, phonetic generalizations,

structural analysis clues;

- poor literal comprehension skills that interfere with answering factual questions; and/or
- poor higher-level comprehension skills that interfere with the ability to engage in abstract analyses.

Strengthening Sight-Reading Skills

When students have difficulty learning sight vocabulary, the source of the difficulty usually is a failure to recognize and recall letter patterns in words (Adams 1990). There are several strategies these students can be encouraged to try.

A Multisensory Approach

One strategy that often works is to use a multisensory approach by: (1) writing the word on a card; and (2) having students trace the word with their fingers (after making sure they are physically able to trace) while simultaneously saying the word. Once students are successful, have them turn the card over, then say and write the word from memory. While this is a slow procedure, it can be very effective for students who can remember and apply these steps to new words—when this occurs, the procedure becomes a learning strategy.

Tracing also provides students with configuration clues that can help them recall the specific letter orders in certain sight words, using the letters' distinctive shapes. Tracing the word helps to reinforce visual recall of the letter patterns. You are not focusing on the shape itself—the outline of the word helps many students to remember letter patterns. For example, as shown in figure 3-1 below, the word *school*, with its distinctive upper "coastline," would be an appropriate word to choose. The word *soon*, which has no distinctive configuration features, would not be an appropriate choice.

Word-Picture Association

Associating a detail in the printed word with a picture also can be helpful for students who have difficulty recognizing and recalling letter

Figure 3-1

Configuration Clues

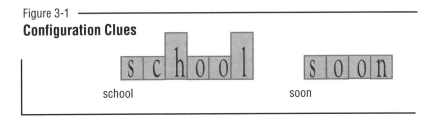

school

soon

patterns in words. For instance, drawing eyes in each *o* of the word *look,* or drawing a woman's face in the *o* in *mother* can aid students' memories. Not surprisingly, when students make these associations on their own and draw pictures to reinforce what they have learned, they remember the word better than if you supply the visual cue.

Word Division

Breaking a large word into smaller, identifiable parts also can be a useful technique in developing sight vocabulary. For example, help students identify the two words that make a new, compound word. Then ask them to guess the meaning of the new word, based on the meanings of the two words with which it is made. If you are teaching phonograms, help students isolate the letters that, together, have the same sound from word to word— like the *eat* in *beat, meat, defeat,* and *retreat.* This technique also is helpful when students are sight-reading plural forms—have students circle or underline each plural's root word.

Visual Scanning

Visual scanning is an effective, practical way to reinforce sight-word identification, particularly for those students who frequently misread or omit word endings and unknown words as they read. Students start by writing several problem words, identified and listed on the board by you, as models. Then students may scan the reading selection to locate and circle the problem words from their lists before reading the passage in its entirety. Visual scanning becomes an even stronger learning strategy when students initiate the process for themselves, identifying and listing their own problem words in a passage, then structuring their own scan, locate, and circle activities for practice.

Simultaneous Reading Activities

Simultaneous reading activities are useful to expand children's vocabulary while increasing reading fluency. A popular version is the neurological impress method (NI), in which the teacher or a designated student instructor (SI) reads a selection aloud along with the student who needs assistance (Heckelman 1969). The instructor points to each word as it is read. If the student stumbles or hesitates, the instructor keeps on reading. This tends to reduce student frustration and self-consciousness while maintaining fluency and improving comprehension. Bos (1982) took this technique a step further with a method of repeated readings, which uses NI as a first step, after which students practice rereading the selection independently until they can read it fluently. At this point, they are ready to respond to comprehension questions. These approaches focus on increasing reading fluency as an aid to comprehension, as well as vocabulary acquisition.

Language Experience Approach

A language experience approach (LEA) allows students to create stories using their own vocabularies—an approach many students find motivating and nonthreatening. A student dictates a story, sentence by sentence, to the teacher, who repeats what was said (correcting syntactic errors) while writing the sentences neatly on chart paper. Stories are read repeatedly to expand the student's instant word-recognition skills. The stories also may be copied by the student to further reinforce the acquisition of newly learned words, because the learning process is strengthened when language experience and a multisensory approach are combined. Sets of stories are sometimes bound into a book, which can be read by others in the class if students choose to share their tales. For students who are reluctant to create their own stories, current song lyrics, holiday songs, or favorite poems can be used to model the process. The goal is to increase the number of repetitions of words in con-text, leading to increased numbers of words in students' sight vocabularies.

Context Clues

For students who need a learning strategy to use context clues, have students: (1) say "blank" when they come to an unknown word; (2) read the sentence aloud—as if they were "talking to someone"—so that both visual and auditory senses are engaged; and (3) focus on identifying known parts of an unknown word. Showing children how to utilize the other words in a sentence to figure out an unknown word helps them focus on comprehending content.

Reading Program

Programmed reading series like the Sullivan Reading Series (Sullivan 1966) or computer programs like Descriptive Reading I & II (Buchter 1996), introduce sight words systematically, with opportunities for students to engage in independent practice and to receive feedback. For students who are able to maintain on-task behavior and check their own work, these programs offer opportunities to work on vocabulary development with little assistance.

Strengthening Phonetic and Linguistic Word-Analysis Skills

Both students for whom English is a second language and students with special needs benefit from simplified, controlled structuring of the

English language to focus on consistencies rather than exceptions. To use phonetic word analysis skills effectively, students must be able to make associations between the printed letter(s) and the corresponding speech sound.

Key Words

For those who find it difficult to associate English symbols with their sounds, a key-word teaching strategy can be helpful because it places the sound in context. To prepare material for this strategy, put the sound on one side of a card and the key word on the other side so youngsters have opportunities for independent practice after the key word strategy is introduced. To teach the strategy, begin by having the youngster say the key word, then the sound in isolation and, finally, the new word. Some guidelines for applying the strategy follow:

1. Only choose key words for sounds the child finds difficult. Key words are especially useful when teaching children short vowel sounds, consistent vowel digraphs (e.g., EA, OA—when two vowels go walking, the first one does the talking), and diphthongs (e.g., OY, OI, OUGH).
2. Select the clearest and simplest key word to illustrate a particular sound. For example, to hear the 'short i' sound at the start of a word, *it* is a better choice than *igloo*.
3. When possible, select key words that interest the students or, better still, have them select their own key words. Youngsters can create a picture to represent the word, as for example, converting the word *it* to the monster of the same name. Some teachers use the *Initial Reading Deck* (Cox 1972) or the *Advanced Reading Deck* (Cox 1980a), both of which contain cards with letter symbols and key word cues, to reinforce instruction and for review.

Visual Cues

Visual cues that employ visual scanning techniques are effective aids for students who are able to associate sounds and symbols but who do not always "see" the letter(s) when they are part of a word. Color coding or bold lettering are commonly used techniques to help children discriminate word parts quickly and effectively. However, they take time to prepare. One way to handle this matter is to have a more advanced student highlight specific problem sounds, print instructional material using specified colors or bold letters, and even act as a student instructor or teaching buddy. Also, sometimes students with special needs can scan, locate, and underline or highlight problem sounds for themselves before they begin to read a passage. Using this strategy alerts students to problem sounds in advance and leads to smoother, more fluent reading. Commercial materials that emphasize the discrimination of word parts, like *Explode the Code* (Hall with Price 1994), also are available.

Phonograms

A knowledge of phonograms (word families) helps students to focus on common word parts as they analyze words using the principle of minimal change. Rhyming, in combination with the visual reinforcement of word similarities, has long been popular for both instruction and practice. Consistency is the key to using this approach successfully. An old favorite for many teachers is the *Remedial Reading Drills* material (Hegge, Kirk, and Kirk 1955). Using a resource like this helps to safeguard against having exceptions—so prevalent in English—slip into the lesson. Ignore exceptions because, in the early stages of teaching phonograms, they can confuse students badly!

Syllable Generalizations

For youngsters who need practice mastering long and short vowel sounds, go back to basics. Have them read only consistent, single-syllable words until they can identify them automatically. Use the combination of the syllable generalizations shown in figure 3-2 on page 44, along with the key-word strategy, to help students attack unfamiliar words (Durkin 1983). Stress that, while rules work most of the time, nothing works all the time.

Prepare an envelope for each syllable generalization, containing many examples, to give students lots of practice pronouncing the syllable. Later, use a mix of the types of words and syllables to help students organize words either by type of syllable or according to whether the words contain long or short vowel sounds. Most importantly, make sure that all the words chosen for these activities are consistent, strong examples of the syllable rule being taught, because exceptions are not a helpful part of initial instruction.

Once single-syllable generalizations have been mastered, move on to two-syllable words, stressing word division and accent. Typically, words are divided into syllables using patterns like V / C V (when one consonant stands between two vowels, the word is usually divided between the first vowel and the consonant—pi / lot, bro / ken) and V C / C V (when two consonants stand between two vowels, the word is usually divided between the consonants—rab / bit, pon / der). Once students learn to divide syllables, accents, macrons, and breves can be taught. For students who seek more of a challenge, try having them find certain syllables in larger words—for example, locating the syllable *por* in words like *important*, *opportunity*, and *Portugal*.

Figure 3-2 ───────────────────────────────────────
Syllable Generalizations

When the (C) is in parentheses, it means that a consonant may or may not be the first sound in the word. The first example for each word/syllable shows the absence of initial consonant.

Syllable	Rule	Key Words
(C) V C	When there is one vowel in a word or syllable and it is not the last letter, the vowel sound is usually short.	it, cat, crush
(C) V	When there is one vowel in a word or syllable and it is the last letter, the vowel sound is usually long.	I, he, hi, go
(C) V C e	When there are two vowels in a word or syllable, the second of which is an "e," and they are separated by one consonant, the final "e" is silent, and the first vowel is usually long.	ate, broke, cube
(C) V C C e	When there are two vowels in a word or syllable, separated by two consonants and ending in "e," the final "e" is silent and the first vowel sound is usually short.	—, bulge, dance
(C) V V C	When two vowels are together in a word or syllable, the first vowel usually has a long sound and the second vowel is silent. (This rule does not apply to special digraphs.)	each, boat, raid

Durkin, D. *Teaching them to read,* 4th ed.
©1983 by Allyn and Bacon. Adapted by permission.

Phonetic Coding

Phonetic coding techniques provide effective practice when a rule-based approach to word analysis is stressed. Start by reviewing the syllable types and word division approaches. Select passages from materials used in the classroom that contain consistent syllable types, and have students code specified words to apply the newly learned rules. Then, have them read the passage, while attending to the word analysis codes. Coding should lead to more fluent reading. References for applying these rules and principles range from the traditional, but still effective *On their Own in Reading* (Gray 1960) to the more sophisticated *Situation Reading* (Cox 1977).

Mnemonic Devices

Sometimes, mnemonic devices can be used to help students analyze new words. Remember using "Roy G. Biv" to recall the colors of the rainbow? Or "Every Good Boy Does Fine" (or "Deserves Favor") to recall the notes in the musical scale? Well, how about an image of "fancy, reciting mice" to aid in remembering that the "soft" sound in the letter *c* usually comes before an *e*, *i*, or *y* (Cox 1984). Anyone can create mnemonics for just about anything! Not surprisingly, students tend to retain best the mnemonic cues they create for themselves.

Nonsense Words

Some educators believe that a real test of word-analysis skills is the student's ability to apply syllabication principles to nonsense words. For example, children who can correctly pronounce nonsense words like *ixnat*, *fets*, or *impake* seem to have mastered sound-symbol associations, syllable division, and accents. To add another twist, you can have students define the nonsense words and put them into sentences. For example, if *ixnat* means "saw," then "Can I borrow your ixnat?" and "Have you seen *The Chain-Ixnat Massacre?*" are possibilities. This activity offers opportunities for creativity and fun for children who can handle the abstraction of using nonsense words.

Affixes

Isolating affixes can also be helpful when students struggle to analyze multisyllabic words. For example, if the prefix "re" and the suffix "ing" in the word *repainting* are lightly boxed, then the base word becomes more manageable. Using visual scanning and cueing techniques to teach common affixes helps students focus on the different parts of the word that contribute meaning. Another way to reinforce the meanings of affixes is to play word games, creating new definitions and usages. This can be especially funny when nonsense words are used—e.g., *refets* or *fetsing*.

Lenz, Deshler, Schumaker, and Beals (1984) developed a structured sequence of steps to identify and isolate affixes—the DISSECT strategy, shown below.

> **D** iscover the context
> **I** solate the prefix
> **S** eparate the suffix
> **S** ay the stem
> **E** xamine the stem, using rules for syllable division
> **C** heck with someone
> **T** ry the dictionary

With this strategy, students first learn the acronym and the step associated with each letter. Then they learn the actions required at each step in the process.

One way students can keep track of the steps is to cross off each step as they complete it. This is a useful strategy for students who know their affixes but need a structure to apply the knowledge in an organized way. Monitoring student progress is a must, however, because children sometimes skip steps that can significantly impact the effectiveness of this strategy.

Semantic and Syntactic Clues

Applying semantic and syntactic clues is useful whether students are exposed to a content-based reading approach or a phonetic/linguistic or rule-based approach. The best results occur when the unknown word is part of the youngster's listening vocabulary, or when direct teaching is used to build new vocabulary. To determine whether the problem lies with semantics or syntax, begin by listening to the student's "guesses" during oral reading. When guesses seem unrelated to the content of the sentence, it is a good bet that the student needs work getting meaning from print (semantics). In this case, filling in blanks, where the omitted words contribute significantly to the meaning of the sentence, forces children to attend to the surrounding context to complete the sentence: "The little white _____ with the long ears and pink nose hopped across the lawn and into the woods."

If, on the other hand, the guesses indicate the student is substituting words that are one part of speech for words that are another—such as articles for prepositions or conjunctions—or misreads verb tenses or affixes that change the word from one part of speech to another, it is possible that you must stress the structure of the English language (syntactics) with sentences like this: "The _____ pool is closed because it is raining." Either multiple choice items (which are easier) or blanks (which require more vocabulary knowledge) may be used.

Strengthening Literal Comprehension Skills

The abilities to remember factual information and details establish important foundations on which to build increasingly complex reasoning skills. To highlight the importance of literal skills, take the student who, after reading a passage, is asked, "Why do you think *that* happened?" To respond, he or she must remember what *that* was and what the things were that led up to *that*. Without recollection of the people, places, or things described in the passage, no response is possible. By focusing on direct teaching techniques to develop literal comprehension skills, we can increase the likelihood that, in time, students will be better able to manage higher-level comprehension skills.

Rehearsal

Rehearsal is an effective tactic to aid in recall. Some students will benefit from reciting what they read—they can whisper under their breath to avoid disturbing others—to reinforce with their auditory senses what they are taking in visually. Though some children may balk at rehearsal, any college student studying for an exam can endorse its effectiveness. Similar to rehearsal, having students retell the important ideas in their own words is another tactic that promotes the retention of recently read material.

Word Limits

When students have difficulty selecting main ideas, one effective teaching strategy is to set word limits on answers—e.g., "Tell me three important key words that you just read." One way to do this is to have them send "telegrams." For example, after reading the sentence, "Fluffy, the white bunny, likes to play with all the children on the block," a child might first highlight the most important words in the sentence, then use the highlighted words to compose a telegram that reads, "Bunny plays with children." The concept of "telegrams" is easily taught when children are "charged" $5.00 per word. To start, it may be necessary for some students to create telegrams for each sentence or paragraph they read—the decision of frequency is made according to students' instructional needs and the complexity of the reading selection. When used as a game, "telegrams" get youngsters to identify important facts, a skill that teaches outlining—a major study skill.

Word limits also assist students in distinguishing essential from nonessential facts, helping them make judgments about the relative importance of the information provided in connected text. Students use a variation of "telegrams" to generate and critique messages from each other to determine if all needed information is included and to delete information that is nonessential. Students benefit from concrete explanations from classmates, as they compare notes about material that is and is not important in a reading passage.

Notations

If it is permissible for students to write in their texts, or for important pages to be copied, many students benefit from making notations in text margins. For example, an important date or time might be noted using a small clock face or a T in the margin. Sometimes even an asterisk can cue the student to attend to an important fact or detail. In addition, numbering lines in the text is a real help for students who have a hard time sequencing important events.

Chapter 3

Strengthening Higher-Level Comprehension Skills

The strategies that follow are particularly effective for students with special needs who have difficulty mastering higher-level comprehension skills. As always, be flexible in your approach, trying different techniques to find the ones that work best for each student.

Reciprocal Teaching

Palinscar and Brown (1983) developed a method called reciprocal teaching to help students improve reading comprehension. The teacher assigns a silent-reading selection and models the following procedure to enhance students' abilities to understand the material:

(1) prompt by asking students to identify the kinds of questions that would be appropriate to the selection;

(2) instruct;

(3) modify the activity if the student is unable to respond correctly;

(4) praise; and

(5) give corrective feedback.

Once students understand the process and are able to generate good questions, they can take turns questioning each other.

Signal Words

Direct teaching strategies are also useful to highlight signal words—vocabulary that aids in comprehension—in passages. Concentrating on ordinal terms—e.g., first, second, and third—and words that provide sequence cues—e.g., then, when, and next—helps students attend to the order in which ideas are presented in the passage. When used in conjunction with other marker words that contribute meaning—e.g., also, however, either/or, consequently, and because—information is provided to help the reader make correct decisions about the main ideas being presented.

Newspaper Strategies

When a newspaper strategy is used, students read a passage to answer structured "wh" questions: who, what, when, where, and why. (How, though not a "wh" question, often is included, too.) Who, what, when, where, and why questions elicit the facts in the story. Some youngsters benefit from referring to a written guide—as they find each answer, they check off the corresponding question on their papers so they do not stray from the facts. As the name implies, the newspaper technique is often used to report news stories. Consequently, news articles are a great source of practice material to reinforce student learning.

Herber (1978) developed an even more structured Herringbone

technique using the "wh" words, in which a large herringbone V is drawn, with each of the six keywords projecting from the sides of the V, along with space to respond. Armed with a visual model to organize the essential facts in a passage, some students with special needs are able to move beyond literal comprehension skills with ease.

Selection Questions

When questions are available at the end of a reading selection, it is useful to have students preview the questions before they begin to read. Sometimes, however, the wording of the questions can be more complex than the passage. When this happens, it is a good idea to preview and paraphrase questions for the whole class. This approach takes little time and gives all students a better chance at accurate reading and responding. Students who need a more specific strategy can highlight or underline key words in the questions to use as guides when reading the passage.

Scanning techniques are useful when attempting to locate specific words, phrases, or paragraphs that relate to questions in a reading selection. Students can use their fingers or index cards to scan, though some may need to be shown how to track from left to right and from the top to the bottom of the page.

Another concrete tactic that couples questions with their answers is numbering the lines of text for speedy reference. After numbering the lines, students read each comprehension question, locate the line(s) of text that contain(s) the answer, and enter the line number(s) next to the question before writing the answer. In this way, locating answers in text is reinforced, and students are better able to explain how they arrived at their answers.

Cloze Techniques

Cloze techniques that rely on the use of surrounding text to capitalize on semantic and syntactic clues are "old faithful" approaches for assessing comprehension that can also be used to improve comprehension. Blanks are substituted for critical words or concepts in the reading passage; sometimes choices are provided to reduce guessing and increase the likelihood of success. If students need added structure, have them highlight the word or words that led to their response. As they progress, choices may be eliminated, though continuing to highlight words that guide their responses remains a good idea, because combining a concrete activity with a learning strategy can increase student success. Keep in mind that when cloze techniques are used, reading material must be targeted at the student's independent level.

Chapter 3

Semantic Mapping

Semantic mapping or webbing, an adaptable graphic strategy that takes many forms, contributes visual structure to reading selections and allows students to see relationships among significant words and concepts (Leverett and Diedendorf 1992). Mapping usually begins with identifying a keyword or main idea, around which supporting details are written to show connections, as illustrated in figure 3-3 below.

Figure 3-3
Semantic Web

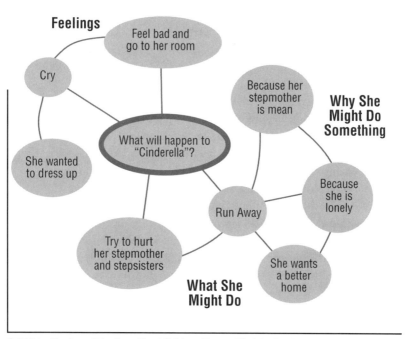

©1992 by The Council for Exceptional Children, Reston, Virginia. Reprinted by permission.

Storyboards

Storyboarding, similar to semantic mapping, is a dynamic approach often used with young children with language deficits. Students identify key elements of a reading selection and either draw or write each element. The drawings or written work are backed with felt, Velcro, or sandpaper and placed on a felt board. Students then arrange and rearrange them until their relationships reflect the reading selection. This hands-on, manipulative approach to organizing concepts is both concrete and effective.

SQ3R

Originally described by Robinson (1941), SQ3R—which stands for survey, question, read, recite, and review—continues to be a particularly productive aid to comprehension. During the survey stage, students skim the advance organizers, turning each heading into a question. Then they read in order to answer the questions. Oral recitation is an excellent way for teachers to assess progress in comprehension, with particular attention to students' abilities to infer, predict, and generalize, based on what they read. Oral responses are typical when SQ3R is first introduced; however, as students become more familiar with the procedure, many prefer to "recite" silently or write their answers. After an entire section or chapter has been read, the questions derived from the headings are again studied to see if students still recall the answers. If not, they reread the sections with which they seem to have difficulty. Direct teaching of each step in the SQ3R process is sometimes needed to assure that students with special needs feel confident using the technique.

Visual Imaging

Visual imaging is a useful tactic to aid students in comprehending short passages. After reading a passage, students close their eyes, picture what they read, and reflect on the content. A brief period of quiet time allows some students to recall and review the content mentally, which promotes comprehension. It is important to monitor this tactic by asking students to describe their visualizations, because there is sometimes a discrepancy between their visual images and reality!

Strengthening Handwriting, Spelling, and Written-Language Skills

Writing sentences consists of a complex array of skills, including oral language, reading, spelling, punctuation, and handwriting, all of which contribute to the final result. Because students with disabilities usually have difficulty in one or more of these areas, it is no wonder that many have a hard time developing written-language skills. Some of the common indicators of learning problems in written language and related areas are:

- difficulty writing legibly and comfortably;
- reading and spelling skills that are significantly below grade level;
- lack of mastery of sentence and paragraph structure, grammar, and punctuation; and
- lack of motivation or an inability to cope with the complexity of the task.

The strategies that follow support the development of written-language skills in students with special needs.

Chapter 3

Handwriting Skills

The motor skills involved in handwriting may present difficulties for students with poor physical coordination. Students who are uncomfortable with the physical aspects of the writing act may be helped by a commercial pencil gripper or a rubber band wound around the part of the pencil gripped by the student. For youngsters who have difficulty writing on a line, commercial products like Right Line (available from Pro-Ed, Austin, Tex.), use raised lines to help students "feel" the line.

Direct instruction in handwriting should be separate from written-language lessons. Instructional strategies include using posted letter models, which students can copy, and models containing color cues and arrows as guides for directionality and for starting and stopping points. An effective, simplified, cursive-writing program, such as the D'Nealian Handwriting Program can also be used (Thurber and Jordan 1981).

Ultimately, for those who lack the basic skills, as well as those for whom writing is, literally, a painful experience, today's technology offers answers in the form of word processing options. After all, signing checks may be the only required handwriting we will need to perform in the twenty-first century—and, with electronic transfers, even that may be unnecessary.

Spelling Skills

Students with special needs sometimes find lessons that combine spelling with writing to be confusing. Consequently, if students demonstrate spelling problems, specific time must be set aside for this activity.

To start, as obvious as it may seem, students must be able to read and understand the meanings of the words they are expected to spell. This may require using direct instruction to teach the words and limiting the number of spelling words assigned at one time.

Some professionals advocate having children use a single learning strategy to study all spelling words. One particularly useful sequence, the Fitzgerald (1951) method, requires students to:
1. Look at the word carefully.
2. Say the word.
3. Visualize the word with eyes closed.
4. Cover the word and write it.
5. Check the word for accuracy.
6. Repeat steps 1 through 5 if the word is misspelled.

A chart that lists each step can be posted to jog students' memories.

Students who have difficulty preparing for spelling tests often find multisensory approaches effective, once they have mastered letter recognition. Students say each letter's name in the word, tracing the letter at the same time. They say and trace several times before writing the word from memory, without a guide.

Applying the syllable rules used for reading to spelling words is a strategy that emphasizes consistent word configurations that follow the rules. For example, the word *take* is an example of a familiar "CVCe" word. Children are urged to "hear" the component sounds in the word. After they look at the word and identify the three sounds, /t/ /ay/ /k/, they are taught to relate the long *a* sound to a silent *e* at the end of the word. The syllable rules may also be applied to spelling longer words. For example, a word like /re/ /mem/ /ber/ can be spelled if students are first shown how to use the syllable rules to segment the word, and if the resulting segments are said slowly so the children can hear the different sounds in the word. The learning strategy, then, has students: (1) say the word very slowly; (2) separate the sounds and/or syllables; (3) write the word; and (4) check accuracy. Many youngsters need to slow down and concentrate on the order in which sounds occur in words before they begin to write; too often, they prefer to rush the task and start writing immediately.

Another approach that focuses on consistent word configurations is word families or phonograms—an especially helpful way to instruct students who possess rhyming and visual-memory skills. For example, in a list that includes *cat*, *mat*, and *sat*, pointing out the "family resemblance"—/at/—may be all that some students require to learn the words. Others may be instructed to highlight the similarities in each word as a preliminary learning strategy.

For students who benefit from attending to details in words, have them sort spelling words into "known" and "unknown" categories, based on word details. Specifically, known words usually are those that are familiar to the youngster (and that follow the syllabication and pronunciation rules), while unknown words are often irregular, deviating from the rules. However, it is the student's ability to spell the word—not the word's adherence to syllable rules—that determines where the word is placed. Using this approach, a spelling list including the words *take*, *grow*, *fair*, and *said* might be reorganized, as shown in figure 3-4 on page 54, to make studying easier. Sorting forces students to study word details carefully. As their word-analysis skills grow, the size of their "known" lists should grow, too. When this approach is used, students concentrate most of their energy on learning words on their "unknown" lists.

Affixes are important word details that contribute to word meaning. When children have a prior knowledge of affixes, they can be guided to box the affixes in words. It is easier to learn the five-letter word *paint* than the eight-letter word *painting*. In addition, this technique helps students see that suffixes rarely change their spellings. It might also be a good time to

Figure 3-4 ───
Reorganized Spelling List: Known/Unknown

Known Words	Unknown Words
take	grow
fair	said

reteach rules for combining base words and suffixes, such as the doubling rule (1:1:1), which says: 1 syllable with 1 short vowel sound and 1 final consonant needs doubling of final consonant before adding the suffix. Therefore:

base word = m/a/p + /p/ (doubling rule) + /ing/ (suffix) = mapping

"Chunking" the parts of the word to be spelled also allows students to focus on word details and reduces the number of individual items to be learned. For example, in the word "string" the groups, or chunks, of letters /str/ and /ing/ are easier to learn than the six separate letters. And, occasionally, using exaggerated pronunciation can help students spell the word correctly and have fun, too. Remember learning how to spell the days of the week? . . . especially "Wed-nez-day"!

Grouping words according to common word parts is another strategy that lets children focus on word details. While this may seem obvious, sometimes these shortcuts must be taught directly to students. For example, the spelling words *vocation, diameter, selection, minister, position,* and *careless* can be reorganized to promote ease in studying, as illustrated in figure 3-5 below. Once they have mastered the strategy of organizing content to capitalize on similarities, students can apply the strategy when studying other subjects.

Isaacson, Rowland, and Kelley (1987) described a totally different approach to spelling that employs a finger-spelling technique based on the manual alphabet used by some individuals with hearing or language impairments. Each of the 26 letters of the alphabet has a specific positioning of the fingers to represent the letter. The positions are also available in easy-to-read chart form. Students who have the manual dexterity required for this approach can use this method to practice their spelling words manually, thus adding a unique multisensory aspect. The authors recom-

Figure 3-5 ───
Reorganized Spelling List: Word Similarities

vocation	minister	careless
selection	diameter	
position		

mended that students begin by dividing each word into parts or syllables and saying each letter orally while finger-spelling it.

A behavioral approach to spelling-in-context can be an incentive for some students to increase the number of correctly spelled words in connected text. When this approach is used, students' spelling errors in written assignments are counted and charted. This technique heightens students' awareness of the importance of spelling in written work and provides a visual record of any improvement. Spelling rewards can be presented to students who decrease their error rates.

When students demonstrate the ability to spell, but their spelling is inaccurate in writing assignments, there is no substitute for proofreading the work. Some techniques for proofreading include going backward through the work starting with the last word, then the next, and the next, and so on, to avoid the distraction of reading for content; delaying proofreading to the next day to create a "window" between writing and proofreading; and having students proofread each other's work. If incorporated as part of formal written-language lessons, it is usually a good idea to set aside a special time for proofreading and editing.

Written-Language Skills

Encoding written language requires a range of skills. Even when students speak in complete and complex sentences, some may be unable to transfer these oral language skills to written work. Using conventional instructional procedures, students can only write what they can read and spell; however, when reading and spelling skills improve, related written language skills often improve as well.

For students who need help using the parts of speech to compose sentences correctly, The *Fokes Sentence Builder* (1992) is an effective classroom tool, providing a structured language approach with picture cards that represent the different parts of speech. Students manipulate the cards to construct sentences, using the structure cues associated with each part of speech. The resulting sentences can be monitored for accuracy and, over time, copied to develop practice with written language. In addition, workbook activities are provided to help students transfer what they learn orally to the printed page.

Based on the Orton-Gillingham approach, Project Read (Enfield and Greene 1987) is a highly structured, multisensory curriculum that incorporates the development of reading, comprehension, and written language skills. The program's written-language component has been used successfully to teach the concept of sentences, as well as sentence-composition skills. After students learn that each sentence is a complete thought, they are introduced to a "writing frame" in which to create a "thought picture."

The basic frame has three parts: the "point" to indicate the beginning word and the need for a capital letter; space for the "thought;" and the punctuation to end the sentence, as shown: /_____. As students become increasingly proficient, symbols are added to show parts of speech, like the subject (—-) and verb (^^^), which look like: /\ _____ + ^^^^^^^. Greater complexity is added when different types of sentences are introduced using this technique, as when punctuation changes from a period to a question mark or an exclamation point. Students using the program have had success "writing orally," which helped develop their understanding of sentence structures. The program also teaches students to diagram sentences in creative and motivating ways to aid their understanding of sentence structure and paragraph development. Project Read's written-language component extends from the end of Grade 1 through Grade 9.

Using visual organizers to structure writing activities can be effective for students whose visual-organization skills exceed their ability to write sentences. Similar to semantic mapping, this strategy first gets students to picture what they want to communicate. They then diagram the main thought, followed by the related details that flesh out the main idea. At its simplest, the main thought (subject and verb) are presented in a center circle, around which spokes are used to communicate details. As increasingly complex writing assignments are undertaken, more complex diagrams can be devised.

Older students can benefit from King's *Writing Skills for the Adolescent* (1985), which contains imaginative ideas to help improve writing skills. In particular, the different types of paragraphs are explained, along with the transition words used to guide the writing of each type of paragraph. For example, when authoring a "classification paragraph," expressions like *first, one type of,* and *the worst* are targeted as useful cues for the reader.

Welch and Jensen (1991) offered a simple strategy that can be used to help students organize ideas into paragraph form using the mnemonic PLEASE, which contains the following steps:

P ick a topic.

L ist ideas about the topic.

E valuate the list of ideas.

A ctivate, using a topic sentence to introduce the paragraph.

S upply supporting sentences.

E nd with a clincher sentence to summarize the paragraph and hold the ideas together.

For some students, the complexity of coping with extensive writing assignments, like reports, may overwhelm them and interfere with their ability to produce, even though they are able to write sentences and paragraphs. With so many competing demands on their energies—formulating ideas, grammar, handwriting, spelling, and punctuation—many students need an orderly process to help them organize and prioritize the many tasks. To address this problem, Bos and Vaughn (1991) outlined a structured writing process that includes:

1. choosing a topic;
2. brainstorming ideas;
3. composing the work;
4. revising and editing; and
5. publishing the final work.

The first two steps can be accomplished in small or large groups, depending on the assignment objective. At the composing stage, diagramming or even creating a semantic web may offer effective alternatives for youngsters who have difficulty putting words on a page. At the revising stage, the focus is on the writing content—specifically, on improving the clarity and continuity of the message. Some questions to ask students—or, when used as a learning strategy, questions that students can ask themselves—as they reread their work for purposes of revision are: Did you pick an interesting, appropriate topic? Did you begin in an interesting way? Did you stick to your topic? Did you include enough/too many details? Does your work make sense? Do you have a good ending? These skills focus on the organization and communicability of the content of the composition. At the editing stage, children attend to language mechanics—grammar, spelling, and punctuation. Finally, the revised and edited work is either rewritten or typed before being submitted to the teacher or shared with other students.

Editing strategies are quite useful in addressing problems with language mechanics. A popular editing guide, devised by Schumaker, Deshler, Nolan, Clark, Alley, and Warner (1981), helps students present their best work by using the mnemonic COPS, which stands for:

C   Have I *capitalized* correctly?
O   How is the *overall* appearance of the paper? Is it well-spaced? Legible? Neat?
P   How is the *punctuation*?
S   How is the *spelling*?

For many of us, getting started is the hardest part of writing. Deciding on a topic and organizing thoughts is often referred to as the planning stage. When students experience difficulty at this stage, structured formats can guide them in their thinking (Vallecorsa, Ledford, and Parnell 1991). By using informal "jot lists" like those shown in figure 3-6 on page 59, students may be less intimidated about the prospect of getting started on their writing assignments.

There are also specific strategies available for particular types of assignments. Graham and Harris (1989) offered the following three-step learning strategy for planning and writing opinion essays:

1. Think, "Why am I doing this? Who will read it?"
2. Plan what to say, using the mnemonic TREE:

   T opic sentence

   R easons

   E xamine reasons

   E nding
3. Then write and say more.

No matter how detailed the strategy, there will be some students who have the ideas and the oral language skills but are unable to put their spoken ideas into written form. They may need to dictate their stories into a tape recorder or to another person who would transcribe the dictation. Then you could grade either the oral presentation or the dictated paper.

For students who possess the necessary writing skills but seem to lack motivation to produce written work, Graham and Harris (1988) recommended several teaching tactics to spark student interest. For example, they suggested talking about the writing styles of various authors as part of the reading assignments. Then, if the reading selection captures their interest, students may be more willing to try their hand at engaging in a similar writing project. Another recommendation is sure to result in a cheer from students: Tell them not to worry about spelling, sentence structure, or other mechanics; tell them just to write. If they are satisfied with their overall results, returning later to "clean it up" may be seen as polishing rather than a punitive measure.

Scheduling a designated writing time each day also helps to make writing "a classroom habit." To demonstrate the fun of writing and its importance in everyday life, make this an activity in which everyone— including you—participates. The amount of time devoted to this activity is less important than the activity itself, so as little as 10–15 minutes may be all that is needed. Possible starter topics from which students may choose are: an article for the school newspaper; a letter to a friend; a note to a classmate; or a diary or journal entry. Whatever the writing activity, students respond most favorably when they select their own topic, when the results are not graded, and when students have assurances that their written work will remain private. If, for example, they write journals, they have a place to express thoughts and feelings without fear of censorship or reprisals. Once the logistics are worked out—for example, allowing students to fold down pages they don't want anyone to read—private journal-writing can be a lot of fun. And, you will be surprised at how eager most students are to share their work with you!

For reluctant authors, Graves and Hansen (1983) recommended

Figure 3-6 ————————————————————————————————————

Formats for Planning Phase of Various Types of Student Writing

Jot List
(Main Ideas)

1._____

(Support) _____

2._____
_____
_____

3._____
_____
_____

Paragraph Planner

Topic Sentence

Supporting Details

Conclusion

The Hamburger Paragraph

Comparison/Contrast
Jot List

Similarities	Differences
_____	_____
_____	_____
_____	_____
_____	_____

Conclusion:

Relationship Planner

Topic:

Fact:

Relate:

Fact:

Relate:

Fact:

Relate:

Conclusion:

using an "Author's Chair" in which students write and take turns reading their work to others in the class. Depending on grade level and maturity, listeners might serve as "critics," giving feedback to the author on content and style. Some students may be inspired to write simply for the honor of being recognized as "Author for a Day." Others may choose the critic's role, in which they are asked to provide a written review of the author's work.

Another motivating activity for budding authors is to designate a corner of the school library as the "Student Author's Area," devoted to students' "published" work—finished writings that have been typed, collated, and perhaps even illustrated. To accomplish a professional end product, teaching students the typing and word-processing skills needed to use a computer is well worth the time it takes. Pride in the appearance of the final product justifies the effort expended. Also, the value of using word processing as an aid to written expression is no secret. While spell-checks and grammar programs do not teach specific skills, they do assist students in encoding written language that can be read. When the ideas students want to communicate take precedence over their manipulation of the tools of language, the word processor provides a solid support. However, because no single approach to mastering the mechanics of language and handwriting will be applicable to all situations or right for all students, you should encourage students to use a variety of strategies.

Chapter 4

Strategies for Teaching and Learning Mathematics

In today's increasingly complex world, people are required to use numbers in many new ways. From technological applications—like programming a microwave oven or using the local bank's automatic teller machine—to calculating housing expenses or forecasting college costs, a knowledge of numbers and the management of numerical principles have become essential for everyday functioning.

Mathematics educators recognize the importance of preparing students with the array of problem-solving and critical-thinking skills they will need to operate in and adjust to a rapidly changing world. However, some children with disabilities find basic mathematics even more of a mystery than reading and language. After all, math uses a different "alphabet" (0, 1, 2, 3, 4, 5, 6, 7, 8, 9) and a different "sentence structure" (e.g., 2 + 2 = 4). In addition, there is a different notational system (e.g., +, -, $), and there are different "rules" that govern mathematical concepts. These are just some of the reasons that students may have difficulty developing the basic computational and problem-solving skills needed for success in mathematics.

Where to Start

Before beginning instruction, it is important to identify students' mathematics strengths as well as their difficulties. The mathematics section of a student's IEP, coupled with consultation with the professional who conducted the evaluation and any teachers who are familiar with his or her work, are good starting points. This combination of resources should give you an understanding of the type of learning difficulty the student is experiencing, as well as the approximate levels at which the student is currently functioning in math. This information—along with a quick, curriculum-based assessment to confirm IEP assessment results and to answer questions like the ones that follow—should help you determine specific areas in which the student needs assistance and where to begin instruction.

- Can the student read and understand the words in the math text, including the written directions?
- Can the student both retain and follow a series of directions in a logical order?
- Does the student comprehend basic mathematical operations?
- Does the student have the spatial and perceptual skills needed to write mathematical symbols and copy computational problems accurately on paper, with numerals arranged in the proper place-value columns?
- Can the student remember the number facts?
- Can the student perform calculations accurately, with and without a calculator?
- Does the student understand the oral and/or written language expressions used in mathematics—particularly in mathematical problem solving?
- Can the student apply relevant mathematical information accurately?
- Can the student estimate?
- Can the student use abstract concepts—even such basic abstractions as place-value notation—to solve complex problems logically?
- Can the student reason, solve problems, and generalize information?
- Does the student have the prerequisite skills needed for the task at hand?

When assessing students' mathematical abilities, it is particularly important to go beyond basic computational skills and evaluate students' understanding of the effects of operations and their ability to problem-solve. An important consideration is whether students are functioning at a concrete level or at a more abstract level of understanding. For example, some secondary-level students with special needs, though capable of complex math calculations, continue to count on their fingers or use concrete marks to assist them. In that case, what could be easier than providing these students with calculators to compensate for their difficulties in memorizing number facts?

Identifying Problems Unrelated to Math

If children misread operational signs—e.g., if they add when they should subtract—have them circle or trace the sign before doing the problem. Then ask the student to identify each sign and explain what steps the sign requires. This will help you determine whether the problem is a mathematics problem in which the student is unable to understand how to perform the operation or a perceptual problem that causes the student to misperceive the sign.

Sometimes, students ignore other visual details, like omitting the decimal point in math problems dealing with money. When this occurs, having students devote time to a formal "work check" process builds accuracy and independence. It also is useful to allocate a specific time during each lesson to review computational results for reasonableness and accuracy and to check the forms in which the answers are presented.

When students demonstrate visual perception problems or have difficulty organizing space on a page, they can experience major math snags unrelated to either computation or mathematical reasoning. For example, the work of students who have to think about the direction in which numbers face or who are unable to write numbers automatically may not accurately reflect their mathematical abilities. For these students, a card complete with numbers and arrows that indicate the correct way to write each number can be placed on each student's desk for ready reference.

Another perception problem unrelated to computational skill is reversing number order, as when a student writes "41" instead of "14," or consistently subtracting a smaller number from a larger number, regardless of whether it is part of the minuend or subtrahend (which could also be a conceptual problem). When students reverse the order of numbers, rechecking strategies that include estimation and consideration of whether the result is "reasonable" are crucial.

Yet another problem associated with directionality occurs when students perform computations and forget the direction in which they must go. These students may benefit from arrows, strategically placed on their papers, to remind them of the correct direction. The direction of the arrow would, of course, depend on the specific operation. Arrows can also be numbered, as shown in figure 4-1 below, to cue the order in which specific operations occur. This strategy becomes increasingly effective as students learn to place their own arrows before moving ahead to compute answers.

Figure 4-1 —————————————————————————
Directionality Arrows
In the problems below, arrows guide the sequence of actions that students need to follow to solve the problem.

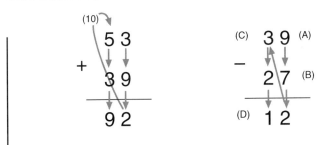

Combining visual perceptual difficulties with poor handwriting can create spatial disorganization, making the resulting work impossible to read, let alone to compute. Try having students perform computations on a piece of lined notebook paper turned sideways, as shown in figure 4-2 below. This technique will help organize the space as students use the lines to keep columns of figures straight.

Figure 4-2
Lined Paper, Sideways
Lined paper guides students to keep numbers in the correct column.

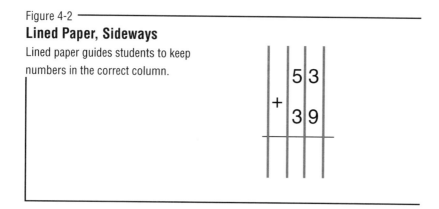

Students can also align columns of figures by using graph paper, an especially helpful technique when focusing on place value. Simply putting one number in each box may help to keep students "in line." For children who have difficulty copying numerical or verbal math problems from the board—when the errors are not due to carelessness on the child's part—you can circumvent the problem by simply providing preprinted worksheets; after all, the objective is not copying, but doing mathematics.

Mastering the Language of Math

For children in Grades K–2 who seem to experience difficulty with either oral- or written-language expressions used in math, the *Boehm Test of Basic Concepts—Revised* (Boehm 1986) offers a screening procedure to assess mastery of approximately 50 terms commonly used in instruction— e.g., few, more, less, over. Once identified, unknown terms can be incorporated into the student's reading, spelling, and written-language lessons to provide added exposure and practice.

For older students with disabilities, direct instruction should be used to teach the key math terms used in each lesson or chapter prior to teaching the skills and concepts contained in the chapter. Word banks, discussed in Chapter 5, that support vocabulary acquisition in subject matter areas provide an organized system with which to learn and review terminology.

For students who experience difficulty reading and understanding directions in textbooks or on math worksheets, one simple approach is to use the problem text as part of direct-reading instruction that focuses on comprehension and fluency. The same approach is productive when students are introduced to mathematical word problems, because word problems typically require reading comprehension, use terms that may be abstract or unfamiliar, and contain a lot of information in compressed form. Consider the following problem from a reading perspective:

> Four friends share a summer house for the month of July. The bills for that month are: $650.00 for rent, $80.00 for food, $50.00 for telephone, and $30.00 for electric. What is the average cost for each friend for the month?

If the problem is not read carefully, the number of people involved might be overlooked. Also, the term *average* in this problem has a particular meaning triggered by the word *each*. From this example, it is easy to see that some students may be able to read every word in a problem and to compute averages but still misunderstand what the problem asks them to solve. By including word problems as part of reading comprehension lessons, terms that are used in ways that differ from conversational usage or that contain words that are not part of the student's mathematics vocabulary can be taught directly, employing strategies similar to those used to teach reading vocabulary. One useful learning strategy that gets youngsters involved is to have them identify and highlight or underline any unknown words they need explained.

Mastering Number Size

If students are overwhelmed by too many numbers in a problem, or by the size of the numbers in a problem, simplification strategies can be used to circumvent the difficulty. For example, look at the following word problem:

> At the local department store, Mrs. Smith bought new winter coats for every member of the family. Mr. Smith's coat cost $88.89, Mary's coat cost $49.99, Phil's coat cost $32.50, and her own coat cost $92.99. How much did the coats cost all together?

One technique that can make the numbers in this problem less intimidating is to demonstrate to students how to simplify the numbers to single digits by examining numbers in the units column, and if the number is above 5, increasing the number in the tens column by one. Thus, Mr. Smith's coat would cost $9.00, Mary's coat would cost $5, Phil's coat would cost $3, and so on. Then students should reread the problem to identify the operation(s) required; calculate the answer using the simplified numbers; solve the problem; and compare the final answer to the answer they received with the simplified numbers.

A more sophisticated simplification strategy, which can be used by older students, involves estimation. Begin by helping students round off each number in the problem to the nearest "10," before attempting a solution. Using the Smith family again, Mr. Smith's coat now costs about $90, Mary's costs about $50, Phil's coat costs about $30, and Mrs. Smith's costs about $90. This approach has the advantage of simplifying initial computations, introducing students to rounding skills as a way to estimate answers and giving them a "ballpark" idea of what their computed solution should be.

Personalizing the problem can also help youngsters relate to word problems. Using the Smith's example once again, students might substitute the names of their own family members for the people in the problem before beginning computations. Anything that helps them identify with what they are doing is a plus!

Mastering Math Facts

Math facts provide a foundation for most types of computation, estimation, and problem solving. When students have persistent difficulty mastering math facts, several teaching and learning strategies are available to circumvent the problem.

Calculators

Once students understand the principles associated with the different mathematical operations, many experts recommend teaching them to use calculators—a skill in itself—because the "bottom line" is an ability to use math as a problem-solving tool. The advantages in using calculators are that they offer a speedy solution to difficulties associated with recalling math facts, and they enable students to proceed to more interesting and varied problems in mathematics, instead of keeping them at the skills level indefinitely. When students understand mathematical relationships and demonstrate the reasoning ability to progress to higher levels of instruction, access to a calculator can build confidence through correct calculations, while at the same time speeding up the computation process.

Concrete Prompts

Sometimes, problems with memorizing number facts can be avoided before they become unmanageable. For example, when number facts are first introduced, allowing children to refer to a facts table may be all the help they need.

For those who require a concrete, physical act to reinforce computing, counting on fingers or using a number line can be useful aids. A number line can serve as a reminder of number sequence. It also can be used to help children count up (add), count down (subtract), or skip-count in groups (multiplication or division). A ruler is an effective and inconspicuous number-line substitute for older students who continue to need a concrete prompt.

Remember that a good sense of direction is a must when using a number line. Therefore, if students seem to have problems with directionality, a number line probably is not the strategy of choice. During a recent educational evaluation, a 7-year-old asked if he could use a number line to solve the math problem "6 - 4 = ?" When I said that was okay, he started at zero, counted to six, then looked at me with a broad smile and said, "Now you just have to tell me which way I go and I can do this problem!" Some teachers express concern that using these aids makes students dependent upon the aids and discourages them from learning the math facts independently. To the contrary, because using aids slows them down, many students are inspired to learn their facts.

Flashcards

Another tool that will help students learn their math facts is that old standby, flashcards. Have students look at the "answer" side of the card and trace and say the problem and its answer. After repeating this activity several times, students can write the problem and the answer on a separate piece of paper—a strategy similar to that used to learn sight vocabulary. Once the math facts have been learned, students with special needs can use the "question" side of the flashcard for added practice.

Computer Programs

Several computer programs are available that reinforce the recall of number facts. These programs often inspire students to stay on task, because many children view computer use as a game or as a reward. In addition, computer programs usually give immediate and dynamic feedback (also a source of reinforcement), and they do not become irritated with a student's incorrect answers!

Finger Math

Students with good manual dexterity and eye-hand coordination may be able to use adaptations of "finger math"—usually complex and intense finger-math instructional programs designed for regular education children. For example, to do a "9 times" fact on your fingers, hold up your hands and number your fingers from left to right, from 1 to 10. If the multiplication fact is "7 x 9," bend the seventh finger down. The six fingers raised to the left of the bent finger is the "tens," and the three fingers raised to the right is the "ones;" hence, the answer is "63." A word of caution: for some youngsters, tactics like this can be just one more disconnected procedure to memorize. If students lack the conceptual understanding, "tricks" like finger math may be more distressing than helpful. Students with left-and-right confusion also would not be candidates for this technique.

Sequencing

Organizing instruction to reduce the amount to be learned makes learning more manageable for many students. For example, when multiplication facts are taught in an organized sequence, children only have to memorize 15 facts (Mercer and Mercer 1993). The teaching sequence is as follows:

1. Teach "0 times any number is 0."
2. Teach "1 times any number is that number."
3. Teach "2 times any number is double that number: 2 x 4 = 4 + 4."
4. Teach "5 times any number involves counting by 5's the number of times indicated by the multiplier: 5 x 4 means 5 (1), 10 (2), 15 (3), 20 (4)."
5. Teach the "9 times" trick by saying "Subtract '1' from the multiplier to get your 'tens'; then calculate the 'ones' by adding enough to the 'tens' number to equal 9: for 9 x 6, subtract 1 from 6 to get the 'tens' (5); then add enough to the 5 to get 9 for the 'ones' (4): (5 + 4 = 9) = 54."
6. The remaining number facts now total 15. They are:
   - 3 x 3 = 9,   3 x 4 = 12,   3 x 6 = 18,   3 x 7 = 21, 3 x 8 = 24,
   - 4 x 4 = 16, 4 x 6 = 24,   4 x 7 = 28,   4 x 8 = 32,
   - 6 x 6 = 36, 6 x 7 = 42,   6 x 8 = 48,
   - 7 x 7 = 49, 7 x 8 = 56,   and
   - 8 x 8 = 64.

Some teachers have even separated out the double-number facts—e.g., 3 x 3, 4 x 4—thus reducing the remaining number facts to be learned to ten! Either way, this becomes a learning strategy when students can identify if the unknown fact: (1) fits one of the categorized types; or (2) must be memorized or counted out.

Count-By

Another approach to assist students with multiplication facts is the "count-by" learning strategy, devised by Cullinan, Lloyd, and Epstein (1981). The five steps in the procedure are:

1. Read the problem: "7 x 5"
2. Point to a number you can count by: "5"
3. Make the number of marks indicated by the other number: " ///////"
4. Count by your number, touching a mark in order each time you count: "5 - 10 - 15 - 20 - 25 - 30 - 35." Stop counting when you touch the last mark.

5. Write the last answer you said: "35."

Mastering Abstract Math Concepts

Abstract mathematical concepts can prove especially difficult for some students. The techniques detailed here can help students with special needs who have difficulty grasping mathematical concepts.

Complementary Operations

Some students benefit from direct instruction in complementary operations—e.g., number-fact families. The realization that they do not have to memorize both "3 + 4" and "4 + 3" as separate facts, and that the answer to "7 - 3" is the same as "4 + ? = 7," has lightened many a student's load. In addition, as students understand the concepts that are the basis for relationships among the four operations, they gain insight into the consistent patterns that exist. For example, students who cannot recall the answer to "8 x 3" have the option to add "8 + 8 + 8." If they cannot remember "27 ÷ 9," they have the option to subtract "9's" from "27" to obtain the answer. Most soon learn the advantage of mastering rapid multiplication and division skills as a way to solve simple computational problems.

Place Value

For students who have difficulty learning place value and regrouping concepts, it sometimes helps to organize the numbers visually, using graph paper. Others may benefit if the underlying numerical organization of the number system is made explicit. For example, if students are taught number sequence as "1 to 10," confusion can result because they may perceive a pattern to the numbers, without comprehending the underlying organization. By contrast, if number sequence is taught as "0 to 9," the relationships that exist among the 10 symbols are clear, as illustrated in figure 4-3 below.

Figure 4-3 ───

Visual Organization of Numbers

0	1	2	3	4	5	6	7	8	9
10	11	12	13	14	15	16	17	18	19
20	21	22	23	24	25	26	27	28	29, etc.

Not only does this sequence stress the base-10 nature of the number system, it also demonstrates consistency through the numeric repetitions. In addition, it highlights the function of zero—an important but difficult concept for many children to grasp.

Manipulatives

Manipulatives, like base-10 materials, are concrete ways to introduce students to the abstract principles of place value and regrouping. Begin by having students build small single- and double-digit numbers with the materials, reinforcing concepts associated with base-10 operations without regrouping. Essential concepts for regrouping are the terms "more than" and "less than" (or their equivalents). As students become proficient, stress the rule that each column on a place-value chart can have no more than nine pieces. Once these concepts are mastered, show that when an addition result in the units column is more than 9, then 10 of those pieces must be "regrouped" with the pieces already in the tens column, and so on. Once the column holds more than 9 pieces, then 10 of the pieces have to be traded for 1 piece of the material in the next place value; thus, 10 unit pieces = 1 tens rod.

As concept development moves to subtraction, demonstrate that if the subtrahend units number is less than the minuend units number, there is also a need to "regroup." Here, however, instead of adding the overage into the tens column, we must break up the 10 in the tens column into 10 unit pieces and place them in the units column of the subtrahend. Color-coding materials to denote units, tens, hundreds, and so on, can be helpful aids for some students, because color concretely reinforces regrouping concepts and processes.

Videodiscs

Bottge and Hasselbring (1993) have successfully brought word-problem concepts to life for elementary children with disabilities using a videodisc program called *The Adventures of Jasper Woodbury*. The videodisc series depicts characters confronted with real-life problems that must be resolved. The combination of action, interest, and reality can motivate children to develop mathematical problem-solving skills because of the more authentic contexts in which the problems are set.

Mastering Problem-Solving Activities

The National Council of Teachers of Mathematics (1989) reviewed curriculum and instructional approaches, then published a set of standards for mathematics education. Among their findings was that, too often, students in regular classes lacked sufficient opportunity to go beyond rote mathematical operations to engage in more abstract problem solving. The *Standards* indicated that too much time was spent on calculation skills and not enough time spent on the development of reasoning skills and their applications. If this is true in regular education, consider the problems faced by students with special needs! Cawley, Baker-Krocynski, and Urban

(1992) recommended that special education promote the new math standards for children with disabilities as well. Thus, across all levels of education, there is a call for students to learn to apply what they know to solve real problems; and there is a corresponding charge for educators to develop the means to make it happen.

Heuristic Strategies

Giordano (1992) proposed the application of heuristic (trial-and-error) strategies to promote the development of reasoning skills—organizational procedures that precede calculation. If heuristic strategies, like the ones that follow, are stressed, teachers' and students' excessive focus on computation skills can be reduced.

- **Annotations.** Before starting to solve the problem, students underline the verbs, bracket the numerical information, and apply other previously taught annotations.
- **Formula Designations.** Before starting to solve the problem that requires a formula, students first write the formula in the margin of the paper.
- **Symbolic Operations.** Before starting to solve the problem, students note and code all the relevant operations.
- **Analogies.** Students create problems similar to the ones assigned by: (1) reading the problem; (2) making up a similar problem; (3) analyzing their problem; and (4) using the same procedure to solve the original problem.

Related to the analogy strategy is a move toward what is called authentic learning. Authentic learning refers to opportunities for students to engage in and master real-life situations, as well as those that resemble real-life. Students are encouraged to manipulate information and ideas in ways that change their meanings and implications (Cronin 1993; Newmann and Wehlage 1993). In this way, instruction goes beyond the classroom and becomes increasingly relevant to students' lives. In fact, having students create a real-life problem similar to one that was assigned is a learning objective in its own right rather than simply a prerequisite step to learning analogies.

Visual Models

Models offer another successful approach to assist students in developing problem-solving skills. When students have difficulty forming a letter or number, we think nothing of posting a model. Why not post math models as well? For example, when using a specific sequence of steps to solve a particular type of math problem, the steps can be posted as reminders. Models make abstract concepts more concrete—and complex problems simpler—because each operation is identified in the order in which it must be performed. Bley and Thornton (1981) reported that using flip charts in which each page shows a single step or stage, or a formula, is particularly effective. It also is possible to detail the complete solution on a single page, which students can then use to check their own work. As with other aids, we have found that children are eager to give up the model quickly; so there is little danger of over-reliance. And, to convert models into a learning strategy, students merely need to "look away!"

Several effective learning strategies can provide models that serve as guides when students solve mathematical problems. Selection of a particular strategy depends on the complexity of the math problem to be solved. One such strategy is the Problem-Solving Prompt Card, devised by Fleischner, Nuzum, and Marzola (1987, 216), shown in figure 4-4 below.

Other step-by-step procedures are available that can be converted to learning strategies to guide students' problem-solving efforts. For example,

Figure 4-4
Problem-Solving Prompt Card

READ	What is the question?
REREAD	What is the necessary information?
THINK	Putting together? + Add
	Taking Apart? – Subtract
	Do I need all the information?
	Is it a two-step problem?
SOLVE	Write the equation
CHECK	Recalculate
	Label
	Compare

©1987 by PRO-ED, Austin, Texas. Reprinted by permission.

an approach that Choate (1990) developed asks students to "study the question" by: (1) scanning for clues; (2) highlighting the clues and the question; (3) revising the question by turning it into a "fill-in-the-blank" statement; then (4) reading the revised statement to research the problem. Such a strategy helps students to approach problems in manageable pieces, aiding greatly in comprehension.

A similar aid to problem solving, devised by Enright and Beattie (1989), uses the mnemonic SOLVE. The strategic steps are:

S tudy the problem.

O rganize the facts.

L ine up a plan.

V erify the plan/computation.

E xamine your answer.

Matrices are a specific type of model used widely in mathematics. Englert and Sinicrope (1994), for example, described a series of matrices that students can use to solve two-digit multiplication problems. A simple example of a matrix for multiplication by one digit is shown in figure 4-5 below. Students can be taught to construct their own matrices, as needed.

Figure 4-5
Matrix for Multiplication

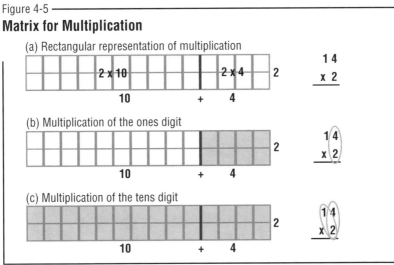

©1994 by The Council for Exceptional Children, Reston, Virginia. Reprinted by permission.

Concern that strategies like finding the key words in a math problem were not consistently successful led Parmar and Cawley (1994) to develop a matrix approach for solving word problems. They suggested teaching word problems around a theme, beginning with simple problems and moving to increasingly complex ones. Students are taught how to use the matrix to solve the problem, and they learn how to refer back to the matrix for future problem solving. For example, 16 two-step word problems were written to exemplify 16 different calculation sequences. The matrix that was devel-

Figure 4-6
Matrix of Problems

| | | First Step | | |
		Addition	Subtraction	Multiplication	Division
Second Step	Addition	1	2	3	4
	Subtraction	5	6	7	8
	Multiplication	9	10	11	12
	Division	13	14	15	16

©1994 by National Council of Teachers of Mathematics, Reston, Virginia. Reprinted by permission.

oped shows the operations needed to complete each problem, as portrayed in figure 4-6 on page 73. Thus, for Problem 1, students would learn that the first step is addition, and the second step is addition; for Problem 7, the first step is multiplication, and the second step is subtraction.

Instead of using a static model, sometimes the class can develop its own sequential set of problem-solving steps inductively. The resulting steps can then be posted for everyone in the class! For example:

- Diagram: Would one be appropriate or helpful?
- Numbers: Jot down the data available.
- Unnecessary information: Analyze the information; if unnecessary, eliminate.
- Key words: Locate and underline.
- Identify operation(s): What procedures are needed to arrive at an answer?
- Type of answer: What is the nature of the required answer? Is it . . . a sum of money? a fraction? a measurement? the area of a shape?
- List steps needed to solve the problem.
- Solve the problem, making sure the answer is expressed in correct terms.
- Check your answer.

Of course, when students develop their own models, they seem to have an easier time remembering them than when the models are imposed externally.

Auditory Models

For students who are primarily auditory learners, taped directions can provide an auditory model to help them master problem solving. To create audiotapes, Wood, Rothenberg, and Carran (1993) suggested that the teacher demonstrate the procedure, talking through each step, while recording the lesson. In this way the teacher provides explicit directions so students know how to replay tapes and follow the verbal cues successfully. Access to the tapes allows students to review previously taught lessons on their own.

Montague and Applegate (1993) recommended an even more basic approach for students who need an auditory model. Students verbalize both the problem and each action that must be taken to solve that problem, using a rehearsal strategy. Initially, you will need to monitor students to make sure that what they say accurately guides their actions. In reality, it is a strategy that many of us use automatically when we're under stress.

Both teaching and learning strategies involve a solid introduction, followed by practice using the strategy, along with monitoring to make sure that the strategy is applied correctly. As students translate math concepts into novel applications, they are well on their way to expanding their problem-solving and reasoning skills.

Chapter 5
Strategies for Teaching and Learning Study Skills

Although students with special needs who attend regular classes for academics like science or social studies may be able to master the course content, they may need to have it adapted or modified in order to read the text and related materials, complete assignments, or take tests. The following strategies focus on advance organizers, vocabulary acquisition, textbook and assignment modifications, and test-taking accommodations, because feedback from regular-class teachers indicates that these essentials influence student success.

Using Advance Organizers

Using a book's advance organizers—the different type sizes, faces, or styles (e.g., bold, italics) that precede passages in text—as an introduction to new subject matter works well for students with special needs, because advance organizers stress important points and frequently introduce new vocabulary. When students are taught to skim material using advance organizers, they gain an overview of the passage or chapter. Skimming can also prevent students from feeling "bogged down" by too much detail at one time. Be certain that, when introducing skimming techniques, reading material is at students' independent reading level. Otherwise, they may focus only on the words they know and be unable to get a real understanding of the content of the reading material. For students who need a concrete learning strategy, writing key words from memory after reading the advance organizers can help. More advanced students might elaborate on the key words to communicate the anticipated content of the text.

Advance organizers also assist students in learning to outline—a study skill commonly used to enhance comprehension. Because this is a labor-intensive activity, a few suggestions follow to make it more palatable for students:

• Save outlining for subject-matter texts in which the advantages—to aid comprehension and facilitate study—are clear.

- Be flexible but consistent about outline formats. Just because we learned to use numerals and letters does not mean that is the only way.
- Students who have difficulty organizing their work in outline form often find that graph paper helps them to organize their notes visually.
- For students who have serious difficulties with spatial organization, you can prepare a partial content outline, with space available for students to augment the outline.

Paraphrasing requires students to use their own words to recall what they read. It also provides insight into whether or not they understand what they read. Paraphrasing may not come naturally to all students—for example, students sometimes try to recite the main idea of a passage verbatim, rather than putting ideas into their own words. Once again, "telegramming" can be an effective tactic when used to build paraphrasing skills. Students begin by identifying key words for the beginning, middle, and end of short passages, then putting the words into sentence order to convey a message. As students become adept, telegrams can become more complex and contain more details. Because it is important for students to receive immediate feedback on the content of their telegrams, cooperative learning groups are a good way to involve several listeners and reactors.

Note-taking, either from lectures or text, offers another way to assist students in recalling information. Because note-taking relies on students' abilities to write and spell, once these skills have been mastered, helping students create a personal notation system can be useful. When making notes from text, for example, special attention may be given to advance organizers. By focusing on major nouns and adjectives, students attend to the important events and details being communicated.

Mastering Content-Area Vocabulary

Because word meanings are essential to comprehension, you may want to have students scan each chapter to locate unfamiliar content-area vocabulary. Students can begin by concentrating on the unknown words contained in the advance organizers, because these words frequently represent important ideas. Leverett and Diefendorf (1992) suggested using a structured vocabulary guide, as shown in figure 5-1 on page 77, to introduce and reinforce new vocabulary. Once students identify unknown words, they can use the text's glossary or a dictionary to find their meanings.

Dictionaries

Making the dictionary a user-friendly tool is an important step, once students have mastered alphabetical sequence. One simple approach to reviewing letter sequence is to have students refer to the letter set that

Figure 5-1

Vocabulary Guide

Word	Pronunciation	Definition	Location
enhance	en-hans´	to make something more valuable, to improve something	(copy the sentence from the book) p. 47, paragraph 3

seems to reside unfailingly atop classroom chalkboards. Another approach uses the *Missing Letter Deck* (Cox 1980b) which contains cards that show letter sequences with one letter omitted. For example, in / __ B C / the initial letter is missing, in / F __ H / the middle letter is missing, and in / S T __ / the final letter is omitted. This type of game-like activity provides useful practice for youngsters who need letter-sequence review.

Quartering the dictionary can make a game out of dictionary use for some students. Once letter sequence is mastered, they can learn to divide the standard dictionary into more manageable parts. Try an experiment. Hold the part of a standard dictionary that contains the word definitions with the book spine down, and open it where you perceive the middle to be. Make sure to bind the extra pages in the beginning and end of the dictionary to the covers with a rubber band. Most of the time, the dictionary will open to words beginning with the letter *m*. Repeat the process with the first half of the dictionary and it will usually open to the letter *e*. When the same procedure is applied to the last half of the dictionary, it typically yields an *s*. Using this process, the four quartiles of the dictionary begin with *a, e, m,* and *s*. If you don't get these results, keep practicing! With practice, before looking up a word, students can use this strategy to determine which quarter of the dictionary they will need, and they can quickly and efficiently open to that section.

Once students have arrived at the appropriate section of the dictionary, paging is used to locate the part of the book that contains the initial letter in the word. Here, students can use their fingers to work forward or backward, until they arrive at words that begin with the same letter as the word they wish to find. For example, if looking for a word beginning with *o*, after opening to the *m* quarter, the student might think: "*m*, followed by *n*, then *o*." Using guide words is a skill that students can employ as they get closer and closer to locating a particular word. You must often show guide words that indicate the first and last word on each page to students and model their use by saying each step in the process aloud. As a teaching strategy, for example, say:

1. I am looking for the word "otter."

2. I'm at the place where words begin with *o*.
3. The guide words on this page are "optimize" and "order" so I need to go forward.
4. The guide words on this page are "outcome" and "outreach," so I must have gone too far.
5. The guide words on this page are "other" and "outclass;" alphabetically "other" comes before "otter," so I must have found the right page.

Making games of having students search for words in the dictionary adds to their confidence as they gain independence and convert the teaching strategy into a learning strategy.

Key Words

Identifying key words is one way to make students aware of the important link between word meanings and content-area reading. Student-created word banks are one effective technique for dealing with key words.

Word banks are created when students write each new word and its definition on an index card, then file it alphabetically in a file box or a loose-leaf binder with alphabetical dividers. Of course, students must have the word bank handy while reading, both for easy reference and for periodic review. For many students, constructing banks of newly mastered vocabulary words represents a real achievement.

When content-area terms have not been mastered, you may need to teach them directly, with plenty of concrete examples. Some teachers preview text content for specialized vocabulary and provide either a quick review of key terms for all students or a one-page glossary of terms for reference. These procedures can reduce confusion for everyone! As you identify specialized content-area vocabulary, students may add the technical terms to their word banks as a way to reinforce newly learned terms. Once content-area vocabulary has been identified, it does not change very much from year to year. This is usually a "one-shot" effort on the teacher's part, and word banks provide a ready means of review for students. Pairing students together as "teaching buddies" also offers a way for them to practice using and reviewing new vocabulary and concepts.

Mnemonic Approaches

Teachers have also used mnemonic approaches successfully to help students learn subject-matter vocabulary. Scruggs and Mastropieri (1990) suggested having students employ a key-word method in which they associate a similar-sounding word with the vocabulary word to assist in remembering the meaning of the new word. For example, if the word "vein" needs to be learned for a health class, associating "pain" from an injection with "vein" may assist in recall.

King-Sears, Mercer, and Sindelar (1992) suggested an IT FITS acronym as a teaching and learning strategy when mastering important science terms:

I dentify the unkown term.

T ell the definition of the term.

F ind a keyword for the term.

I magine the definition doing something with the key word.

T hink about the definition doing something with the key word.

S tudy what you imagined until you know the definition.

Sometimes, it is not enough for students to study unknown vocabulary words. When the reading level of the text is too high, one step you can take is to contact the book publisher to learn if a simplified version of the text is available. Adapted texts, which parallel traditional subject-matter texts as much as possible while controlling reading levels, may also be available. The *Science for You* series (Wick, Nordstrom, Major, and Cresswell 1979) is an example of an adapted textbook approach to learning.

Modifying Text Content

Educators have devised several learning strategies to assist students in using textbooks efficiently. Keep in mind that these strategies are most useful when: (1) the name of the strategy (mnemonic) and the steps are thoroughly taught; (2) the strategy is practiced in well-structured and well-supervised learning situations until it is thoroughly mastered; and (3) the strategy is applied with classroom materials and monitored by either the teacher or a teaching buddy. The ultimate value of any learning strategy is the student's ability to generalize it from one learning situation to others. Teachers who have used the following strategies attest to their value in enhancing the study skills of many students in their classes—not only those with disabilities.

The CAN DO Strategy

The CAN DO strategy, devised by Ellis and Lenz (1987), helps students to remember content information. The mnemonic CAN DO stands for actions in which the students engage:

C reate a list of items to be learned.

A sk yourself if the list is complete.

N ote the main ideas and details using a tree diagram.

D escribe each component and how it relates to others.

O verlearn main concepts, then supporting details.

Chapter 5

The PANORAMA Strategy

Another approach is Edwards's (1973) PANORAMA, a three-stage strategy with substages, designed to provide students with a structured way to approach reading and learning new material:

Preparatory Stage

> **P** urpose for reading (Why am I reading this material?)
>
> **A** dapt reading rate to material
> (Read phrases, not words. Identify keywords in the passage. Identify what the author is trying to communicate.)
>
> **N** eed to pose questions
> (Preview questions at the end of the material. Create questions by turning topic sentences into questions to be answered by reading the text.)

Intermediate Stage

> **O** verview to determine organization
> (Scan and identify advance organizers to help focus on important content.)
>
> **R** ead (Relate reading to purpose and questions.)
>
> **A** nnotate ideas and keywords (Outline important content.)

Concluding Stage

> **M** emorize
> (Use rehearsal, mnemonics, and other means to connect newly learned information to prior knowledge.)
>
> **A** ssess efforts
> (Ask: How'd I do? What did I do well? What can I improve?)

Chapter Outlines

Chapter outlines, organized to highlight key concepts and principles, help students attend to what is important in a chapter. One advantage to using this tactic is that it effectively communicates learning expectations to students. Study guides often include chapter outlines in addition to definitions, study questions, assignment specifications, and evaluation criteria. While time-consuming in their initial development, you can frequently reuse outlines and study guides for several years because, in many areas, the content does not change greatly from year to year.

Text Structure Maps

An option that capitalizes on scan, highlight, and preview strategies uses text structure maps (Grossen and Carnine 1992). These maps, extensions of semantic maps for reading comprehension, employ signal words—e.g., when, however, as a result—to focus students' attention on main ideas and their interrelationships, as well as important details contained in the text. Blank maps that illustrate suggested structures for various types of content are shown in figure 5-2 below.

Introduce the maps by distributing copies of the descriptive map—the most basic map format—to students, along with a carefully chosen text selection that features a clear main idea, several subordinate ideas, and details. After students master using the maps, and see the value of mapping content as a study aid, they often want to branch out and create their own structure maps that are responsive to different kinds of reading material.

Figure 5-2

Blank Text Structure Maps

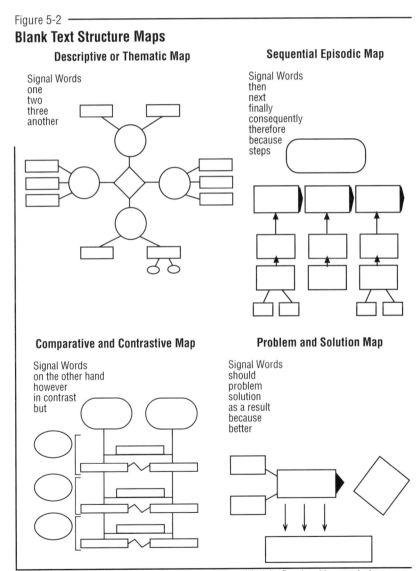

Descriptive or Thematic Map

Sequential Episodic Map

Comparative and Contrastive Map

Problem and Solution Map

Text-Mastery Strategies

For students who are unable to read the text but can comprehend the content of the course, try compensatory text-mastery strategies. One straightforward approach is to have another person read the material aloud while these students follow along, or to have them listen while classmates read the material orally. They might also listen to a tape recording of the content covered in the text, or an abbreviated taped version of the material. While tapes are useful—especially when several students can use the recordings—initial preparation of these recordings requires a major time commitment. The caveat here is that students with whom you use these interventions must have excellent listening and auditory-memory skills, and an adequate ability to take notes and read what they have written, because they cannot refer back to the text.

Graphic Organizers

You can adapt graphic organizers—useful aids in translating written ideas to concrete visual representations—according to subject. Graphic organizers may be developed by the teacher, by small groups of students working together, or by the students with special needs themselves. A sample, structured, graphic overview from a science unit (Leverett and Diefendorf 1992) is presented in figure 5-3 below.

Figure 5-3 ─────────────────────────────
Structured Overview

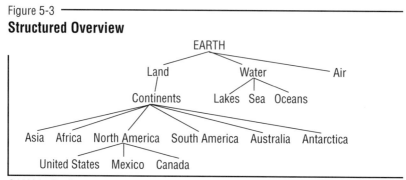

©1992 by The Council for Exceptional Children, Reston, Virginia. Reprinted by permission.

Modifying Assignments

For students who are capable of reading the text but experience frustration when confronted by long assignments, using skim, scan, highlight, outline, or preview strategies can help them focus their reading. Another option is to help youngsters develop the skill of dividing a large assignment into more manageable segments.

Students with disabilities often have difficulty understanding, structuring, and completing assignments, because each of these tasks can seem enormous to them. When they have the prerequisite skills needed to complete an assignment but fail to do so, students may need learning strategies to organize both their time and their work.

Hoover and Patton (1995) discussed many time-management skills that can help make assignments manageable, and addressed such other important topics as note-taking, test-taking, and report-writing. In the time-management section, the authors have devised a sample Daily Time Management Form, shown in figure 5-4 below, in which students identify the major tasks they plan to do and estimate the time it will take to complete each task. The authors also include a helpful checklist so teachers can determine if a student needs a more intensive time-management intervention.

Figure 5-4

Daily Time Management Form

Name: _____

Date:_____Day: _____

Primary Tasks	Estimated Time to Complete Task	Time of Day to Complete Task	Time Task Begun/ Completed	Actual Time to Complete Task

©1995 by PRO-ED, Austin, Texas. Reprinted by permission.

Preparing for and Taking Tests

Studying for tests is hard work and can be the undoing of some students with special needs. These strategies will help students develop the study skills necessary to prepare for test-taking.

Association

Learning theorists have found that an ability to associate newly learned information with previously learned material contributes greatly to retention of the new information. When these connections are made, students have a better chance of being able to store the knowledge in long-term memory and retrieve it when needed. For example, when asked to recall the names of known animals, youngsters whose experiential backgrounds include visits to the zoo are able to "relive" going from cage to cage, remembering the names of animals they saw on a recent visit. These foundations must be developed for students who have limited experiences on which to draw. Examples of ways to lay experiential foundations include taking the class on field trips, using videos to simulate experiences, and having students make word associations to help them remember the sound(s) a letter makes.

Visualization

Visualization can also aid memory, when students are familiar with the object or information to be visualized. Experiential background and a student's ability to recall prior experiences play an important part in determining the usefulness of this strategy. Have children look at the material to be learned, then either close their eyes or look away and "picture" the new material in their minds. Then have students, either orally or in writing, relate what they remember from their visualization and follow up by reviewing the original content to check for accuracy.

Rehearsal

Because memorization is the strategy of choice for many students, the following are provided as tried-and-true memory enhancers. Repeating the information to be learned over and over is a simple technique called rehearsal. When used to learn how to spell a word, for example, students reproduce the letter sequence aloud several times before writing it. For students who benefit from using multisensory approaches, a repeated look-say-write procedure may be needed to learn the material. Some students recopy class notes not only for neatness, but also because recopying helps them remember the content that was covered. Though many people are able to use rehearsal techniques with ease, some children—especially those with disabilities—may need you to demonstrate the strategy concretely in order to master it.

Chunking

Chunking is a variation on rehearsal in which you group the material to be remembered into logical segments. A good example is Social Security numbers—who among us can recite his or her number without the two pauses? When students are taught to chunk the material to be learned, there are fewer separate elements to remember. Students can then devote the time saved to rehearsing the material they must memorize. Applied to spelling, the process might look like this:

Rather than trying to memorize the six-letter word *string*, divide

the word into two letter groupings: *str* and *ing*.
By reducing the amount of material to be learned to two chunks, it is easier to memorize.

Mnemonics

Mnemonics are frequently used memory enhancers, as shown by the number we have included in this book. One approach uses the first letters of the list of items to be memorized; for instance, given this list of living things—snake, python, lizard, asp, toad, tadpole—students can create the acronym SPLATT! When students generate their own mnemonics, they usually remember them better; and making a game out of finding the "perfect" mnemonic can be a lot of fun!

An especially useful mnemonic designed to help students with disabilities to prepare for tests is the EASY strategy (Ellis and Lenz 1987), which includes the following steps:

E licit "wh" questions—who, what, when, where, why—to identify important information.

A sk yourself which information is the least troublesome or difficult.

S tudy the easier material first and the harder material last.

Say "**Y** es" to self-reinforcement—give yourself a reward!

With this strategy, too, working as part of a cooperative learning group is an effective way to have students drill each other to reinforce memorized information. Practicing with peers offers real reasons to repeat the material with opportunities for feedback. Alternatives that involve the student as teacher include "teaching" the cat, or talking into a tape recorder. Be sure to monitor the "teacher" regularly, however, to make sure that the information being rehearsed is accurate.

The SPLASH approach, created by Simmonds, Luchow, Kaminsky, and Cottone (1989), is an excellent learning strategy for students to apply to test-taking. Here, students are instructed to:

S kim the entire test. Note directions, easy and hard questions, and the relative point values so you can use time to best advantage.

P lan your strategy, once you have a general idea of the test.

L eave out difficult questions in a planned manner. Cue students to mark skipped items with an asterisk.

A ttack the questions you know immediately.

S ystematically guess, after exhausting other strategies. Instruct students to look for clues and answers on the test to help answer unknown questions, if there is no penalty for guessing.

H ousecleaning—leave 5–10 percent of the allotted time to make sure that all answers are filled in, all erasures are cleaned up, and all answers are checked.

Chapter 5

Remember, these types of teaching and learning strategies are only effective if they are carefully chosen to be consistent with students' abilities, and taught in a systematic and structured way. If students see value in using the strategies—especially if the strategies result in higher grades and real progress—you can be sure that they will not resort to old ways like cramming, giving up, or skipping class!

Chapter 6

Strategies for Teaching and Learning Social, Communication, and Mobility Skills

While some students with disabilities may, with support, successfully meet the academic demands of the regular classroom. However, these same students may have difficulty with social, communication, or mobility skills. Strategies for strengthening these three areas are described in this section.

Improving Social Skills

Although some students with disabilities may meet the academic challenges of the regular classroom, they may have difficulty socializing appropriately with peers. This difficulty can lead to social isolation. Because making and keeping friends are important skills for living, we have included several effective approaches to improve the overall quality of social interactions in the classroom.

Preschoolers and young children often benefit from affirmation activities—for example, teacher behaviors like smiling and offering positive personal statements to the students (McEvoy, Shores, Wehby, Johnson, and Fox 1990). At the start, you can adapt songs and games to focus on pleasant social interactions. After the children have absorbed the strategy and get used to hearing positive comments about themselves, activities can focus on having students use affirming statements with each other, which converts this into a learning strategy.

Buddy systems are generally easy to implement. Students may be paired for social situations like snack time, with the expectation that peer modeling will occur to foster desired social behaviors. You can implement this strategy most effectively when you generate a list of actions for the members of each buddy team to follow—actions that take each team beyond mere physical proximity. For example, learning how to make small talk together, exchanging information on a topic of current interest, or learning a new social skill might be activities that a buddy team might address. If buddy teams become part of the culture of the classroom, the entire class could get involved in developing and expanding the list as a group project. To have broader impact on the class, you can reconstitute the teams on a regular basis or restructure them to suit different social purposes.

Another strategy, the peer support committee, uses a more structured approach to improving social interactions (DiMeo, Ryan, and DeFanti 1989). Committee members can either be elected by peers or selected by the teacher to serve for a specific term. Members work together to solve social problems that occur for individuals or groups in the classroom. For example, the peer-support committee might offer assistance to a newcomer in making a friend; suggest a "study buddy" for another classmate; or identify a social supporter for a particularly shy classmate. If all students in the class have a chance to participate on the committee, and all students also have the chance to be helped, there will be no stigma attached to needing a little "extra" something. Vaughn, McIntosh, and Spencer-Rowe (1991) recommended using a suggestion box so that students can identify problems anonymously. In this way, individuals who feel the need for some form of social support can even refer themselves! Combining the two techniques can provide an effective network of support for all members of the class.

A related problem-solving strategy, designed to avert social problems (Vaughn et al. 1991), uses the mnemonic FAST:

> **F** reeze! Think to yourself, What is the problem?
>
> **A** lternatives! Do I have some different choices?
> Think of at least two.
>
> **S** olution! What solution should I choose?
>
> **T** ry the solution. If it fails, go back to "**A.**"

Advantages to teaching this strategy are that students learn to: (1) slow down long enough to identify that they have a problem; (2) analyze the problem and generate possible options using their reasoning abilities; and (3) learn to trust their judgment, as they act independently to solve social issues before they become social problems.

Several published programs that address the social problems of students with special needs have the advantage of being adaptable for use in regular classes. One example is *Asset* (Hazel, Schumaker, Sherman, and Sheldon-Wildgen 1981), designed for use with adolescents. The program focuses on eight social skills that have been identified as important attributes of successful interpersonal interactions:

- Giving positive feedback;
- Giving negative feedback;
- Accepting negative feedback;
- Resisting peer pressure;

- Problem-solving;
- Negotiation;
- Following instructions; and
- Conversation.

Instructional materials and teaching directions accompany this program, and it is quite user-friendly, which is a bonus for teachers when dealing with this complex area.

Improving Communication Skills

Some students who attend regular classes are unable to communicate using oral language. Their problem may be due to difficulty with hearing, speech and language, cognition, cerebral palsy, or some combination of motor impairments. Educators have successfully used alternative or augmentative communications systems to assist these students in communicating with both teachers and peers. Miller (1993) classified these systems as either aided—requiring some sort of physical device to facilitate the communication process—or unaided, relying on hand and body movements alone.

Communication Boards

Communication boards, an example of an aided device, run the gamut from paper constructions to highly sophisticated technological creations. Typically, teachers may use any type of flat surface to hold overlays of one or more pictures or symbols, or a series of symbols. Because the boards are customized to meet users' needs, symbolic representations can range from very basic ones—e.g., food, bathroom—to complex language structures that are needed for high-level, two-person communication in the classroom and beyond.

Recent high-tech innovations work like computers. For example, portable, lap-size communication aids come with sophisticated voice output capabilities that allow a youngster to communicate "verbally," and a pressure-sensitive keyboard for those who have dexterity problems (available from Crestwood Company, Milwaukee, Wisconsin).

Selection of a board depends on the individual's level of functioning and command of language—determinations usually made by an interdisciplinary team of professionals, including a speech and language clinician. At one extreme, a student might simply be able to point to a desired item using the pictures on the board. At the other extreme, students who possess both receptive and expressive language skills use their communication boards to send and receive complex messages.

When students who use communication boards are placed in your classroom, communication relies on understanding what the keyboard

symbols mean. The symbols must be translated into language that everyone—the student with special needs, the regular-class students, and you—
understands. If a standard symbol set such as *Blissymbols* (Silverman,
McNaughton, and Kates 1978)—shown in figure 6-1 below—is used, it is
probably necessary for an interpreter or facilitator to be available to assist
the student and you—at least at the outset.

Figure 6-1

Sample Blissymbols

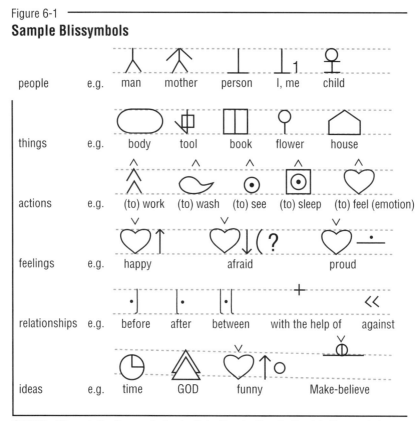

©1978 by Blissymbolics Communication Institute, Toronto, Canada. Reprinted by permission.

Sign Language

Sign language, an example of an unaided language system, consists of
a series of manual signs that represent language. American Sign Language
(ASL) is the language of the deaf community in the United States and
English-speaking Canada and is, therefore, used most frequently in those
areas. ASL is not a manual version of English but a separate language with
its own form and syntax—for example, a single sign can be equivalent to an
entire phrase or concept in spoken language. As a result, some students
who use sign to communicate may manifest idiosyncratic English-language

difficulties in written work.

Finger spelling associates different finger positions with each letter of the alphabet, requiring the "speaker" to spell each word. Although too slow to be used for interactive communication, finger spelling is helpful to communicate single words or short messages.

To limit feelings of isolation when students who use sign are placed in a regular classroom, teachers and peers often learn the basics of sign to communicate with their new classmates—and because it is fun to learn a new language! Sometimes peers go well beyond the basics, creating social communication options with the students with disabilities. However, if you conduct much of your classroom instruction using lecture and discussion methods, students who communicate mainly by sign often need an interpreter in class with them.

Lipreading

Reading the speaker's lips—called either lipreading or speech reading—is another technique individuals who cannot receive messages primarily by hearing may use. Students who use speech reading to gain content information in the classroom should be seated at the front of the room where they can see the teacher clearly, with the "better ear" positioned to take in whatever sound is possible. It is important to face these students when speaking—avoid giving directions while facing the board, for instance—and to keep your mouth uncovered so that these students have an unobstructed view of your lips. In addition, speak naturally. If you exaggerate your speech, you will distort the way you produce the sounds, making the "listener's" speech-reading job even more difficult, because most English-language sounds are extremely difficult to discern from lip and mouth movements alone. If you have a student in your class who speech-reads, you will need to learn the specific accommodations that he or she requires.

Gesturing

Nonverbal children with severe impairments sometimes use gesturing, another form of unaided communication, to communicate their wants and needs. In addition, you can often teach these individuals to respond to conventional gestures. When this is the desired outcome, it may be necessary to ask the special-education teacher to identify particular gestures that are used by and/or for a specific individual.

Improving Mobility Management

Legally mandated environmental adaptations, such as ramps or handrails, are important additions to school buildings and classrooms, because they permit students with mobility problems to gain access to education in appropriate settings. Once in the classroom, a variety of adaptive equipment is available for these youngsters. Usually prescribed by the child's doctor, physical therapist, or occupational therapist according to specific needs, equipment can range from wheelchairs for non-ambulatory students to braces for support and artificial limbs for functional and cosmetic purposes.

When preparing for a student with mobility-management difficulties to become part of the class, two important considerations are: (1) adequate aisle space for maneuvering; and (2) room to store the student's adaptive equipment. For students who have demonstrated an ability to handle the regular-class curriculum and have already learned to use their adaptive equipment, a key to acceptance by classmates may be demystifying their mobility issues. This step is usually taken with the agreement and assistance of the child with special needs. Like so many of us, children are fearful of what they do not understand. Removing the mystery about a child's disability can provide a real opportunity to focus on individual differences and diversity in positive ways. Perhaps peers can use simulated activities to experience what it is like to be physically challenged. This is the part of your curriculum that might emphasize empathy, patience, tolerance, and a resulting appreciation of diversity.

Part III. Conclusions and Reflections

Getting Results

In most ventures, we measure success in relation to the results we obtain. Whether we are learning to surf the Internet, collaborate with other teachers, or select the right strategy for the right student at the right time, it is the outcome that matters. We begin Chapter 7 by summarizing several of the particularly important points about strategies, students with disabilities, and you, which then leads to a discussion of the use of strategies in relation to the premises that we stated in Chapter 2. From there, we take some time to explore the power of collegial approaches to consultation, collaboration, and cooperation as enabling tools for making instruction more effective for all students. Finally, we close with some reflections about the role you may play in changing education, now and in the future, through life in your classroom.

Reviewing Selected Highlights

First, the educational setting, professionals, peers, and instructional strategies must be considered when a student with special needs is placed into a regular-education class. When the blend of talents, attitudes, values, and competencies "works," the result is a successful outcome for everyone—the student, his or her peers, and the teachers.

Second, to identify a starting point for instruction, we suggest reviewing the student's records, communicating with colleagues who have worked with the student, and talking with the student. You should use curriculum-based assessment as the foundation for the program that the student with special needs will follow.

Third, we use the term *strategy* broadly, differentiating teaching strategies from learning strategies inasmuch as both are important instructional tools. We have included a representative selection of research-based strategies to start you on your way to teaching students with special needs. And, because we focus on how students function rather than how they are "labeled," we emphasize strategies that are generic rather than disability-specific—though we have included disability-specific tips for teachers in the appendix on pages 101–3.

Fourth, although usable with any student, these strategies often make the difference in how students with disabilities fare in the regular class-room. When you make necessary adjustments to assignments, tests, or some other aspect of instruction, these students have a greater likelihood of being able to function effectively in the class.

Finally, we discuss the importance of making educational decisions that are consistent with the views and values of your school and district, while remaining true to your personal philosophy of education. Specifically, we discuss strategies that you may follow in directing each student in your class on a course to meet the goals of education.

Reviewing the Premises

The educational challenges that you face daily are multiplied when your classroom is composed of increasingly diverse groups of students. It is our fervent hope that these challenges have also become a synonym for "opportunities." To assist you in making the most of your opportunities, we return to the premises with which Chapter 2 began—you might want to go back to pages 15–16 to reread them—to create a checklist against which you can measure students' progress toward "getting results." We have derived several questions and probes from each premise to provide you with a self-study checklist.

At the end of the day, ask yourself . . .

The Goals of Education

- Were today's short-term curriculum objectives immediately useful or relevant to students? Could they apply them to some aspect of life right now? Did I provide any opportunity for students to practice the skills in a real-world context?
- Do today's curriculum objectives provide foundations on which to build future knowledge? Do the objectives relate to the real world in which students will live when they graduate from school?
- Do these curriculum objectives contribute to students meeting the goals of education in the years following school? Will each goal or objective help students to function personally, participate socially, or contribute economically?

Individual Differences

- Did the curriculum objectives I selected allow me to address each student's individual differences in ability, aptitude, prior experiences, and

interests?
- Did the instructional strategies I selected allow me to address each student's individual differences in ability, aptitude, prior experiences, and interests?

Placement
- After reviewing how the student with special needs performed in class today, did he or she have a positive educational experience? Do I believe that this student can succeed in my class? If I have reservations, why do they exist? Are there objective reasons?
- On whom can I rely for assistance? Who are the professionals with whom I can share concerns, collaborate, and cooperate?

Program
- Is my classroom an appropriate place for each student educationally? Does each student have the ability to meet the goals of education through exposure to the regular-class curriculum? Do any students require specific accommodations to either the curriculum or the instruction? Can these students meet the goals of education if the accommodations are provided?
- Is my classroom an appropriate place for students socially and psychologically? Does each student relate to specific classmates in positive ways? Are there classmates who relate each student positively? Are there discernible friendships that have formed? Does each student have the social communication skills to get along with peers? Does each student seem at ease in the setting? Does each student seem to "fit in"?

Professional Integrity
- Have I maintained my own professional standards?

Building Students' Foundations

Just how important are the goals of education? From our perspective, these goals should guide every educational decision teachers make—decisions like what to teach, and why, how, when, and where to teach it. In a relatively few years of schooling, it is important to build foundations that will last a lifetime for all students. In particular, these foundations have a profound impact on the quality of life that students with special needs ultimately experience.

Because students have a finite amount of time in which to gain the knowledge, skills, and competencies they need to fulfill the goals of education, time is valuable! Using time effectively with students, and especially with students with disabilities, makes the difference between successful outcomes of schooling and results that do not quite hit the mark. Thus, it is up to educators to make sure that time is spent wisely and well, with the long-term interests of students always in view.

Getting Results through Consultation, Collaboration, and Cooperation

Making effective use of the time that students with special needs spend in school poses unique opportunities for educators. Today, public education is shifting from the autonomy that characterized teaching in schools in the United States through the 1970s (Lortie 1975). One reason for this shift is that physical separation—in which one adult interacts almost exclusively with a group of children for about seven hours a day—was one aspect of the isolation that teachers faced. Other factors were a reluctance to share problems and seek advice, borne of "the sense in isolated settings that to seek advice from other teachers is to admit, at least to some degree, a lack of teaching competence" (Rosenholtz and Kyle 1984, 12).

However, there has been in recent years a significant shift to more collegial behavior among educators, as they move from roles characterized by isolation, autonomy, and independence to roles that require and favor consultation, collaboration, and cooperation. This movement toward interdependence was fueled, at least in part, by the growth of the resource room as a special-education delivery-system option that required both regular and special educators to teach students with mild disabilities in their regular-education classes.

Consultation

Friend (1988) argued that consultation developed its roots as a service-delivery option in the late 1960s and '70s—timing that coincides with the advent of resource rooms. From inception, educators have made efforts to clarify and refine concepts associated with consultation, collaboration, and—more recently—cooperative teaching. Common themes that appear to characterize these approaches are: trust building, collegial sharing of values and problems, reciprocity and mutuality, and joint responsibility for all stages in the process, from problem identification to the evaluation of outcomes.

Early consultation efforts were frequently seen as hierarchical—situations in which regular educators who needed assistance working with students with special needs went to special educators. This apparent imbalance in the relationships between professionals led Johnson and Pugach (1992) to differentiate the consultant role as "expert" from the collaborative role as "colleague."

Chapter 7

Collaboration

To break away from the expert model of consultation, Idol, Paolucci-Whitcomb, and Nevin (1986) proposed a model of collaborative consultation in which there is reciprocity between individuals who mutually work to define problems and create solutions. Within this context, Johnson and Pugach (1992) identified four roles that they asserted are played by participants in consultative activities—roles that determine power relationships among them: (1) the prescriber; (2) the informer; (3) the facilitator; and (4) the supporter. Depending on who plays which role at what time, anyone can be either a consultant or a collaborator, according to this model.

Regardless of each participant's role, however, Voltz (1992) observed that problem solving is central to collaboration among colleagues. With that in mind, she recognized that a systematic approach to the process was required and proposed the use of the CLASP model, outlined below, so that all participants have needed opportunities to share actively in the problem-solving process:

C larify the problem.
L ook at the array of factors that influence the problem.
A ctively explore available options.
S elect the best option.
P lan to implement the option.

Cooperation

Bauwens, Hourcade, and Friend (1989) identified a related form of collaboration, focused exclusively on the in-class relationships between regular and special educators: cooperative teaching or co-teaching. Cooperative teaching represents the implementation phase that follows problem identification and program planning and that includes team teaching, complementary instruction, and supportive learning activities. Subsequently, Bauwens and Hourcade (1991, 20) described each of these activities in detail:

> In a team-teaching arrangement, a common body of subject content is a shared instructional responsibility between the two cooperative teachers. . . . In complementary instruction, although the general educator maintains primary responsibility for teaching specific subject matter, the special educator provides instruction in specific strategies or skills to all students who might benefit from such assistance. . . . Supportive learning activities refer to activities that supplement the essential instructional content of presented lessons.

Therefore, both professionals share responsibility for planning, instruction, and evaluation of outcomes.

Bauwens and Hourcade (1991) also identified several important procedures that participants in cooperative-teaching endeavors must clarify when initiating cooperative-teaching activities:

1. the specific cooperative-teaching arrangements—i.e., exactly who does exactly what, and when;
2. scheduling;
3. classroom organization and overall management;
4. classroom rules and discipline techniques;
5. joint planning time;
6. student and parent communication;
7. paperwork responsibilities;
8. program monitoring;
9. assignment of grades; and
10. acquisition and utilization of materials and equipment.

While some activities are easier than others to resolve, all of the items are important because, if not considered, any one of them can lead to miscommunication. Miscommunication in collaborative consultation relationships can be costly, because communication is the cornerstone of collaboration (Pugach and Johnson 1995).

Among the benefits of collaborative consultation and cooperative teaching as they are practiced today are the following:

- growth of mutual trust, esteem, and feelings of professional self-worth;
- feelings that teaching provides ongoing opportunities for renewal and growth;
- increased sharing of professional concerns about real classroom issues and educational needs;
- improved initial teaching and continuous teaching improvement; and
- mentoring opportunities, with the chance to share expertise.

However, Reeve and Hallahan (1994, 9) noted that "the decision to use collaborative methods in the classroom as a means to deliver services to identified and at-risk students must be based on the assurance that this form of service delivery will best serve these students by improving their academic, social, and behavioral standing." This admonition reminds us all that we must base every educational decision, including efforts at collaboration and consultation, on the goals of education and the needs of students. While this notion is true for all students, we must make it the cornerstone of education for students with special needs. We must also be certain to plan for, monitor, and evaluate these decisions and their outcomes continually, making necessary adjustments in the interest of students' learning (Reeve and Hallahan 1994).

Reflecting on the Future

The debate about placements for students with special needs continues. As society's priorities change, laws also change. For example, presently there are competing forces at play between the government's responsibilities to protect individual rights and the role of the government to protect the rights of individuals with disabilities. Today, consideration of proposals to deregulate education, to shift funding for most educational programs to states in the form of block grants, and to expect all children to meet challenging educational standards are among the immediate changes that may be on the horizon. These comprise the next phase of opportunities for us all as we move into the next millennium.

Combining Student Characteristics with Instruction: Tips for Teaching[1]

Each of the different disabilities to which we refer in this guide is, in its own right, a field of study with firm foundations in its own literature and research. In Part II, we included generic strategies to use with youngsters who demonstrate a variety of special needs. Here, we present some disability-specific tips, adapted by permission from Smith and Luckasson's *Introduction to Special Education: Teaching in an Age of Challenge* (1995) that may also be useful. Remember that, while you can use many of these tips with any student, they provide indispensable support for students with disabilities who need them to function effectively in your classroom.

Mental Retardation

- Make sure you have students' attention before you begin.
- Select learning activities that are functional and relevant to students' educational needs.
- Teach skills under the most realistic conditions possible.
- Use concrete materials to introduce new skills, before using representations and abstract oral language.
- Provide plenty of opportunity for students with deficits in short-term memory to rehearse and practice new skills.
- Use varied, interesting materials when reviewing newly learned information.
- Involve students actively in the learning process.

Behavior Disorders/Emotional Disturbance

- Establish clear rules for the class.
- Role play and practice rules with the students.
- Reinforce students when they show appropriate behavior.
- Be sure that the consequences for following or not following rules are fair.

---

[1]Adapted by permission from Smith, D. D., and R. Luckasson. 1995. *Introduction to Special Education: Teaching in an Age of Challenge*, 2d ed. Needham Heights, Mass.: Allyn and Bacon.

- Foster cooperation and friendship by teaching students how to work together in small groups.
- Teach students skills to negotiate and mediate conflicts independently.
- Find at least one thing to praise each student for every day.
- Keep accurate records of behavior changes that occur when medication is adjusted.

Learning Disabilities

- Teach students strategies to help them organize, comprehend, and remember information.
- Include activities that encourage students to think and solve problems.
- Focus students' attention on the relevant features of a task.
- Use concrete examples, often demonstrating how to perform the task correctly.
- Individualize instruction, allowing students to master skills at their own rate.
- Engage students actively in their own learning.
- Help students understand the connection between effort and success.
- Have students predict the consequences of their behavior.

Speech or Language Impairments

- Incorporate activities that allow students to practice skills mastered in speech/language therapy sessions.
- Designate space in the classroom—perhaps a large, round table—that is earmarked for sharing and discussion activities.
- Create a supportive environment in which students are encouraged to communicate with each other, exchange ideas, and discuss topics of interest.
- Plan activities in which students use oral language for different purposes—e.g., making a speech, leading a discussion.

Visual Impairments

- Position the student's desk close to the blackboard and near the teacher's desk.
- Place the student's desk away from a light source but in a well-lighted area to reduce glare.
- Free the classroom of dangerous obstacles; remove clutter.
- Open or close doors fully, because a half-open door can be dangerous.
- Put materials in the same place consistently so students know where to locate materials they need.
- Eliminate as much unnecessary classroom noise as possible, because the ability to hear what is going on is essential for these students.

- Encourage students to express their visual needs.
- Explain the explicit and implicit rules of games and social situations.
- Provide plenty of opportunities for students to interact with their sighted peers.

Hearing Impairments

- Position the student as close to the speaker as possible.
- Make sure that any aids the student uses are in working order.
- Spend time talking to the child alone so that you become accustomed to each other's speech.
- Reduce background noise in the classroom as much as possible.
- Articulate clearly, speak slowly, and make sure your mouth is visible. Use an overhead projector instead of a blackboard so students can see your mouth.
- Restate information frequently by paraphrasing.
- Avoid moving around the classroom while talking.

Physical Disabilities or Health Impairments

- Make sure that all areas of the room and school are accessible to students.
- Make sure that instructional materials and leisure activities are within reach.
- Use materials and activities that are appropriate for the student's chronological age.
- Assure personal privacy if assisting the student with hygiene.
- Post emergency instructions and telephone numbers where they are readily accessible.
- Stay alert for signs of fatigue in the student.
- Lift only as much weight as you can.

References

Adams, M. J. 1990. *Beginning to read: Thinking and learning about print.* Cambridge, Mass.: MIT Press.

Armstrong, T. 1994. *Multiple intelligences in the classroom.* Alexandria, Va.: Association for Supervision and Curriculum Development.

Bauwens, J., and J. J. Hourcade. 1991. Making co-teaching a mainstreaming strategy. *Preventing School Failure* 35(4): 19–24.

Bauwens, J., J. J. Hourcade, and M. Friend. 1989. Cooperative teaching: A model for general and special education integration. *Remedial and Special Education* 10(2): 17–22.

Bergan, J. R. 1977. *Behavioral consultation.* Columbus, Ohio: Merrill.

Bley, N. S., and C. A. Thornton. 1981. *Teaching mathematics to the learning disabled.* Rockville, Md.: Aspen Systems.

Boehm, A. E. 1986. *Boehm test of basic concepts-revised.* San Antonio, Tex.: Psychological Corporation.

Bos, C. S. 1982. Getting past decoding: Assisted and repeated readings as remedial methods for learning disabled students. *Topics in Learning Disabilities* 1(1): 51–57.

Bos, C. S., and S. Vaughn. 1991. *Strategies for teaching students with learning and behavior problems,* 2d ed. Boston: Allyn and Bacon.

Bottge, B. A., and T. S. Hasselbring. 1993. Taking word problems off the page. *Educational Leadership* 50(7): 36–38.

Brandt, R., ed. 1987. Staff development through coaching. *Educational Leadership* 44(5).

Brophy, J. E., and T. L. Good. 1986. Teacher behavior and student achievement. In *Handbook of research on teaching,* 3d ed., ed. M. C. Wittrock, 328–75. New York: Macmillan.

Buchter, C. 1996. Descriptive reading I and II. Freeport, N.Y.: Educational Activities.

Cawley, J. F., S. Baker-Krocynski, and A. Urban. 1992. Seeking excellence in mathematics education for students with mild disabilities. *Teaching Exceptional Children* 24(2): 40–43.

Choate, J. S. 1990. Study the problem. *Teaching Exceptional Children* 22(4): 44–46.

Cox, A. R. 1972. *Initial reading deck.* Cambridge, Mass.: Educators Publishing Service.

Cox, A. R. 1977. *Situation reading: Clues to the code.* Cambridge, Mass.: Educators Publishing Service.

Cox, A. R. 1980a. *Advanced reading deck.* Cambridge, Mass.: Educators Publishing Service.

Cox, A. R. 1980b. *Missing letter deck.* Cambridge, Mass.: Educators Publishing Service.

Cox, A. R. 1984. *Structures and techniques: Multisensory teaching of basic language skills.* Cambridge, Mass.: Educators Publishing Service.

Cronin, J. F. 1993. Four misconceptions about authentic learning. *Educational Leadership* 50(7): 78–80.

Cullinan, D., J. Lloyd, and M. H. Epstein. 1981. Strategy training: A structured approach to arithmetic instruction. *Exceptional Education Quarterly* 2(1): 41–49.

Davis, J. 1992. Transition to teaming. *Instructor: Middle Years* 2(2): 16–18.

Deshler, D. D., E. S. Ellis, and B. K. Lenz. 1996. *Teaching adolescents with learning disabilities: Strategies and methods,* 2d ed. Denver: Love Pub. Co.

DiMeo, J., L. Ryan, and A. DeFanti. 1989. Activating collective expertise through collaborative consultation: Classroom alternatives support teams. Paper presented at the meeting of the Council for Exceptional Children, San Francisco.

Durkin, D. 1983. *Teaching them to read*, 4th ed. Boston: Allyn and Bacon.

Edwards, P. 1973. PANORAMA: A study technique. *Journal of Reading* 17(2): 132–35.

Edwards, C., and J. Stout. 1989–90. Cooperative learning: The first year. *Educational Leadership* 47(4): 38–41.

Ellis, E. S., and B. K. Lenz. 1987. A component analysis of effective learning strategies for LD students. *Learning Disabilities Focus* 2(2): 94–107.

Enfield, M. L., and V. Greene. 1987. *Project read: Report form and story form reading guide*. Bloomington, Minn.: Language Circle Enterprises.

Englert, G. R., and R. Sinicrope. 1994. Making connections with two-digit multiplication. *Arithmetic Teacher* 41(8): 446–48.

Enright, B., and J. Beattie. 1989. Problem solving step by step in math. *Teaching Exceptional Children* 22(1): 58–59.

Fitzgerald, J. A. 1951. *The teaching of spelling*. Milwaukee, Wisc.: Bruce.

Fleischner, J. E., M. B. Nuzum, and E. S. Marzola. 1987. Devising an instructional program to teach arithmetic problem-solving skills to students with learning disabilities. *Journal of Learning Disabilities* 20(4): 214–17.

Fokes, J. 1992. *Fokes sentence builder*. Columbus, Ohio: SRA/McGraw-Hill.

Forest, M., and E. Lusthaus. 1989. Promoting educational equality for all students: Circles and maps. In *Educating all students in the mainstream of regular education*, ed. S. B. Stainback, W. C. Stainback, and M. Forest, 43–57. Baltimore: P. H. Brookes.

Friend, M. 1988. Putting consultation into context: Historical and contemporary perspectives. *Remedial and Special Education* 9(6): 7–13.

Fuchs, D., P. Fernstrom, S. Scott, L. Fuchs, and L. Vandermeer. 1994. Classroom ecological inventory: A process for mainstreaming. *Teaching Exceptional Children* 26(3): 11–15.

Fullan, M. 1990. Staff development, innovation, and institutional development. In *Changing school culture through staff development—1990 ASCD yearbook*, ed. B. R. Joyce, 3–25. Alexandria, Va.: Association for Supervision and Curriculum Development.

Fullan, M. G., with S. M. Stiegelbauer. 1991. *The new meaning of educational change*, 2d ed. New York: Teachers College Press.

Gardner, H. 1983. *Frames of mind: The theory of multiple intelligences*. New York: Basic Books.

Giordano, G. 1992. Heuristic strategies: An aid for solving verbal mathematical problems. *Intervention in School and Clinic* 28(2): 88–96.

Goldstein, H. 1974. *Social learning curriculum, Level 1*. Columbus, Ohio: Merrill.

Goldstein, H. 1975. *Social learning curriculum, Level 2*. Columbus, Ohio: Merrill.

Goldstein, H. In process. A plan for reform in the education of mildly retarded students: The curriculum gap - Realization and resolution.

Gottlieb, J., M. Alter, and B. W. Gottlieb. 1991. Mainstreaming academically handicapped children in urban schools. In *The Regular Education Initiative: Alternative perspectives on concepts, issues, and models*, eds. J. W. Lloyd, N. N. Singh, and A. C. Repp, 95–112. Sycamore, Ill.: Sycamore.

Graham, S., and K. R. Harris. 1988. Instructional recommendations for teaching writing to exceptional students. *Exceptional Children* 54(6): 506–12.

References

Graham, S., and K. R. Harris. 1989. Improving learning disabled students' skills at composing essays: Self-instructional strategy training. *Exceptional Children* 56(3): 201–14.

Graves, D. H., and J. Hansen. 1983. The author's chair. *Language Arts* 60(2): 176–83.

Gray, W. S. 1960. *On their own in reading: How to give children independence in analyzing new words*, rev. ed. Chicago: Scott, Foresman.

Grossen, B., and D. Carnine. 1992. Translating research on text structure into classroom practice. *Teaching Exceptional Children* 24(4): 48–53.

Hall, N. M., with R. Price. 1994. *Explode the code*, 6th ed. Cambridge, Mass.: Educators Publishing Service.

Hardman, M. L., C. J. Drew, and M. W. Egan. 1996. *Human exceptionality: Society, school, and family*, 5th ed. Needham Heights, Mass.: Allyn and Bacon.

Hasazi, S. B., A. P. Johnston, A. M. Liggett, and R. A. Schattman. 1994. A qualitative policy study of the least restrictive environment provision of the Individuals with Disabilities Education Act. *Exceptional Children* 60(6): 491–507.

Hazel, J. S., J. B. Schumaker, J. A. Sherman, and J. Sheldon-Wildgen. 1981. *ASSET: A social skills program for adolescents*. Champaign, Ill.: Research Press.

Heckelman, R. G. 1969. A neurological impress method of remedial reading instruction. *Academic Therapy Quarterly* 4(4): 277–82.

Hegge, T., S. Kirk, and W. Kirk. 1955. *Remedial reading drills*. Ann Arbor, Mich.: George Wahr.

Herber, H. L. 1978. *Teaching reading in content areas*, 2d ed. Englewood Cliffs, N.J.: Prentice-Hall.

Hoover, J. J., and J. R. Patton. 1995. *Teaching students with learning problems to use study skills: A teacher's guide*. Austin, Tex.: PRO-ED.

Idol, L., P. Paolucci-Whitcomb, and A. Nevin. 1986. *Collaborative consultation*. Rockville, Md.: Aspen.

Isaacson, A. G., T. P. Rowland, and P. A. Kelley. 1987. A fingerspelling approach to spelling. *Academic Therapy* 23(1): 89–96.

Janney, R. E., M. E. Snell, M. K. Beers, and M. Raynes. 1995. Integrating students with moderate and severe disabilities into general education classes. *Exceptional Children* 61(5): 425–39.

Johnson, L. J., and M. C. Pugach. 1992. Continuing the dialogue: Embracing a more expansive understanding of collaborative relationships. In *Controversial issues confronting special education: Divergent perspectives*, ed. W. C. Stainback and S. B. Stainback, 215–32. Needham Heights, Mass.: Allyn and Bacon.

Johnson, R. T., D. W. Johnson, and E. J. Holubec. 1987. *Structuring cooperative learning: Lesson plans for teachers*. Edina, Minn.: Interaction Book Co.

Jones, V. F. and L. S. Jones. 1986. *Comprehensive classroom management: Creating positive learning environments*, 2d ed. Boston: Allyn and Bacon.

Joyce, B., B. Showers, and C. Rolheiser-Bennett. 1987. Staff development and student learning: A synthesis of research on models of teaching. *Educational Leadership* 45(2): 11–23.

King, D. H. 1985. *Writing skills for the adolescent*. Boston: Educators Publishing Service.

King-Sears, M. E., C. D. Mercer, and P. T. Sindelar. 1992. Toward independence with keyword mnemonics: A strategy for science vocabulary instruction. *Remedial and Special Education* 13(5): 22–33.

Lazzari, A. M., and J. W. Wood. 1993. Reentry to the regular classroom from pull-out programs: Reorientation strategies. *Teaching Exceptional Children* 25(3): 62–65.

Lent, J. 1975. *Project MORE (Mediated Operational Research for Education): Toothbrushing.* Redmond, Wash.: Edmark.

Lenz, B. K., D. D. Deshler, J. B. Schumaker, and V. C. Beals. 1984. *Learning strategies curriculum: The word identification strategy.* Lawrence: University of Kansas Institute for Research on Learning Disabilities.

Leverett, R. G., and A. O. Diefendorf. 1992. Students with language deficiencies: Suggestions for frustrated teachers. *Teaching Exceptional Children* 24(4): 30–35.

Lortie, D. C. 1975. *Schoolteacher: A sociological study.* Chicago: University of Chicago Press.

McEvoy, M. A., R. E. Shores, J. H. Wehby, S. M. Johnson, and J. J. Fox. 1990. Special education teachers' implementation of procedures to promote social interaction among children in integrated settings. *Education and Training in Mental Retardation* 25(3): 267–76.

Mercer, C. D., and A. R. Mercer. 1985. *Teaching students with learning problems,* 2d ed. Columbus, Ohio: Merrill.

Miller, J. M. 1993. Augmentative and alternative communication. In *Instruction of students with severe disabilities,* 4th ed., ed. M. E. Snell, 319–46. New York: Merrill.

Montague, M., and B. Applegate. 1993. Middle school students' mathematical problem solving: An analysis of think-aloud protocols. *Learning Disability Quarterly* 16(1): 19–32.

Muncey, D. E., and P. J. McQuillan. 1993. Preliminary findings from a five-year study of the Coalition of Essential Schools. *Phi Delta Kappan* 74(6): 486–89.

National Council of Teachers of Mathematics. 1989. *Curriculum and evaluation standards for school mathematics.* Reston, Va.: NCTM.

Newmann, F. M., and G. G. Wehlage. 1993. Five standards of authentic instruction. *Educational Leadership* 50(7): 8–12.

Odden, E. R., and P. Wohlstetter. 1995. Making school-based management work. *Educational Leadership* 52(5): 32–36.

Palinscar, A., and A. L. Brown. 1983. Reciprocal teaching of comprehension-monitoring activities: Technical report no. 269. Champaign: Center for the Study of Reading, University of Illinois at Urbana-Champaign.

Parmar, R. S., and J. F. Cawley. 1994. Structuring word problems for diagnostic teaching: Helping teachers meet the needs of children with mild disabilities. *Teaching Exceptional Children* 26(4): 16–21.

Phillips, V., and L. McCullough. 1990. Consultation-based programming: Instituting the collaborative ethic in schools. *Exceptional Children* 56(4): 291–304.

Pugach, M. C., and L. J. Johnson. 1995. *Collaborative practitioners, collaborative schools.* Denver: Love Pub. Co.

Reeve, P. T., and D. P. Hallahan. 1994. Practical questions about collaboration between general and special educators. *Focus on Exceptional Children* 26(7): 1–10, 12.

Reynolds, M. C., M. C. Wang, and H. J. Walberg. 1987. The necessary restructuring of special and regular education. *Exceptional Children* 53(5): 391–98.

Robinson, F. P. 1941. *Effective study.* New York: Harper and Row.

Rosenberg, M. S., L. O'Shea, and D. J. O'Shea. 1991. *Student teacher to master teacher: A handbook for preservice and beginning teachers of students with mild and moderate handicaps.* New York: Macmillan.

References

Rosenholtz, S. J., and S. J. Kyle. 1984. Teacher isolation: Barrier to professionalism. *American Educator* 8(3): 10–15.

Safran, J., and S. P. Safran. 1985. Organizing communication for the LD teacher. *Academic Therapy* 20(4): 427–35.

Salend, S. J. 1994. *Effective mainstreaming: Creating inclusive classrooms*, 2d ed. New York: Macmillan.

Salend, S. J., and C. Hankee. 1981. Successful mainstreaming: A form of communication. *Education Unlimited* 3(3): 47–48.

Salend, S. J., and D. Viglianti. 1982. Preparing secondary students for the mainstream. *Teaching Exceptional Children* 14(4): 137–40.

Schumaker, J. B., D. D. Deshler, S. Nolan, F. L. Clark, G. R. Alley, and M. M. Warner. 1981. Error monitoring: A learning strategy for improving academic performance of LD adolescents (Research report no. 32). Lawrence: Kansas University Institute for Research on Learning Disabilities.

Scruggs, T. E., and M. A. Mastropieri. 1990. Mnemonic instruction for students with learning disabilities: What it is and what it does. *Learning Disability Quarterly* 13(4): 271–80.

Semmel, M. I., T. V. Abernathy, G. Butera, and S. Lesar. 1991. Teacher perceptions of the regular education initiative. *Exceptional Children* 58(1): 9–24.

Showers, B., B. Joyce, and B. Bennett. 1987. Synthesis of research on staff development: A framework for future study and a state-of-the-art analysis. *Educational Leadership* 45(3): 77–87.

Simmonds, E. P. M., J. P. Luchow, S. Kaminsky, and V. Cottone. 1989. Applying cognitive learning strategies in the classroom: A collaborative training institute. *Learning Disabilities Focus* 4: 96–105.

Silverman, H., S. McNaughton, and B. Kates. 1978. *Handbook of Blissymbolics*. Toronto, Canada: Blissymbolics Communication Institute.

Slavin, R. E., ed. 1989. *School and classroom organization*. Hillsdale, N.J.: L. Erlbaum Associates.

Slavin, R. E. 1989–90. Research on cooperative learning: Consensus and controversy. *Educational Leadership* 47(4): 52–54.

Smith, D. D., and R. Luckasson. 1995. *Introduction to special education: Teaching in an age of challenge*, 2d ed. Needham Heights, Mass.: Allyn and Bacon.

Stainback, S. B., W. C. Stainback, and B. A. Ayres. 1996. Schools as inclusive communities. In *Controversial issues confronting special education: Divergent perspectives*, 2d ed., ed. W. C. Stainback and S. B. Stainback, 31–43. Needham Heights, Mass.: Allyn and Bacon.

Sullivan, M. W. 1966. *The Sullivan reading program*. Palo Alto, Calif.: Behavioral Research Laboratories.

Thurber, D. N., and D. R. Jordan. 1981. *D'Nealian handwriting*. Glenwood, Ill.: Scott Foresman.

U.S. Department of Education. 1993. *15th annual report to Congress on the implementation of IDEA*. Washington, D.C.: USDE.

Vallecorsa, A. L., R. R. Ledford, and G. G. Parnell. 1991. Strategies for teaching composition skills to students with learning disabilities. *Teaching Exceptional Children* 23(2): 52–55.

Vaughn, S., R. McIntosh, and J. Spencer-Rowe. 1991. Peer rejection is a stubborn thing: Increasing peer acceptance of rejected students with learning disabilities. *Learning Disabilities Research and Practice* 6(2): 83–88.

Voltz, D. L. 1992. Just what do you mean, "collaborate"? *Learning Disabilities Forum* 17(4): 32–34.

Welch, M., and J. B. Jensen. 1991. Write, P.L.E.A.S.E.: A video-assisted strategic intervention to improve written expression of inefficient learners. *Remedial and Special Education* 12(1): 37–47.

Wick, J. W., C. D. Nordstrom, S. T. Major, and J. H. Cresswell. 1979. *Science for you.* Adapted textbook series. Austin, Tex.: Steck-Vaughn.

Will, M. C. 1986. Educating children with learning problems: A shared responsibility. *Exceptional Children* 52(5): 411–15.

Wolery, M., D. B. Bailey, and G. Sugai. 1988. *Effective teaching: Principles and procedures of applied behavior analysis with exceptional students.* Boston, Mass.: Allyn and Bacon.

Wood, D. A., M. S. Rothenberg, and D. T. Carran. 1993. The effects of tape-recorded self-instruction cues on the mathematics performance of students with learning disabilities. *Journal of Learning Disabilities* 26(4): 250–58, 269.